Teen Speak

About the Author

Jennifer Salerno, DNP, CPNP, FAANP is a nurse practitioner, author, speaker, and founder of Possibilities for Change (PossibilitiesforChange.com). She has practiced for over 20 years as a nurse practitioner working with diverse adolescent populations and has served as a board member and adviser for many state and national organizations and initiatives to improve adolescent health. This work opened her eyes to the prevention effort needed to reduce serious injury and premature death rates in teens.

In keeping with her favorite quote attributed to Mahatma Gandhi, *"Be the change you wish to see in the world,"* Jennifer founded Possibilities for Change and set out to develop user friendly tools and trainings for health-care professionals to use to quickly identify risky teen behaviors and provide effective counseling to reduce those risks. She received the Society for Adolescent Health and Medicine Hilary E.C. Millar Award for Innovative Approaches to Adolescent Health Care for her work in developing the nation's leading adolescent risk screening system: the Rapid Assessment for Adolescent Preventive Services (RAAPS).

Dr. Salerno understands that health professionals aren't the only ones concerned about helping adolescents navigate the teen years – parents have the biggest influence. Further fueled by a passion to also help parents connect with their teens on important risks like substance use, sex, and mental health-related issues, she authored this book to help ensure that parents have the support and resources they need to handle the challenges of raising a teen.

When not working to improve adolescent health, Jennifer loves *family time* exploring the country biking, hiking, and skiing with her husband, daughter and son.

■ ■ ■

Teen Speak

'*Teen Speak* brings much-needed science to the complex task of parenting teens. Dr. Salerno's real life scenarios and practical suggestions reflect her professional expertise as a nurse practitioner who has cared for many teens and guided preventive care improvements among clinicians and public health professionals. This book offers numerous techniques that aim to transfer healthy decision making skills from parent to teen. A must read for all parents!'

— *Margaret McManus, The National Alliance to Advance Adolescent Health*

'*Teen Speak* is a valuable resource for parents. More importantly it provides ways for parents to develop the skills to connect with their adolescents, helping them to become "askable" parents.'

— *Barb Flis, Parent Action for Healthy Kids*

'*Teen Speak* is the closest thing to an owner's manual for parents of teenagers. They will find insight about their developing teens and practical advice and guidance on how to support healthy parent-teen relationships. A must read for every parent!'

— *Dr. Terri D. Wright, American Public Health Association*

'*Teen Speak* offers a valuable roadmap to navigate the rewarding yet challenging transitions involved in parenting adolescents. By integrating experience, evidence, and empathy, this book provides a strategic framework to achieve meaningful dialogue and healthy relationships between teens and parents.'

— *Dr. Fred D. Rachman, Alliance of Chicago Community Health Services*

'*Teen Speak* provides excellent techniques for talking with teens and finding ways to adapt our approaches to avoid conversational dead ends. I plan to use these with my patients and my sons.'

— *Dr. Steve North, Family Physician and Adolescent Medicine Specialist*

'A must read book for any parent of a pre-teen or teen! *Teen Speak* offers practical, easy to understand strategies for improving communication and strengthening your relationship with your teen.'

— *Carrie Tarry, Adolescent Health Coordinator, State of Michigan and parent of two teenage sons*

'*Teen Speak* provides practical advice and explanations for parents to help teens navigate the challenges in adolescent years. The book expands on Dr. Salerno's pioneering work building positive research-based programs for teens and communities.'

— *David Yeung, ETR Associates*

Teen Speak

A guide to understanding and communicating with your teen

Dr. Jennifer Salerno

Illustrations by Nathalie Ghioni

Library of Congress Control Number: 2016909746
Possibilities for Change LLC, Dexter, Michigan, USA

ISBN: 0997701307
ISBN-13: 978-0997701302

Contents

Section 3: Avoiding Common Pitfalls

Acknowledgements

I would like to express my sincere gratitude to the many people who provided support, talked things over, read, offered comments, allowed me to quote their experiences and assisted in editing, proofreading and design—thank you! I am blessed with a tremendous amount of support and assistance from family, friends and colleagues, and I owe the success of this book to all of you. I wish to personally thank those who spent countless hours assisting me with completing the final draft: Adam Bolan, Ariel Cribbins, and Kristine Nash-Wong.

Above all I want to thank my husband, Dave, for standing beside me throughout my career. Thank you for reading every draft, talking each chapter over with me, and offering suggestions to make this book even more parent friendly. Thank you for supporting and encouraging me in my work to improve adolescent health, despite all the time it takes my attention away from home. I would like to dedicate *Teen Speak* to my husband and two beautiful kids, Jordyn and Bryce, and to all the parents working to build strong relationships with their teens.

If even one parent can understand their teen better, identify their risky behaviors and communicate with their teen in a real, productive way—then this effort was worth it! Thank you to everyone for helping to make my dream a reality.

■ ■ ■

Foreword

I know what you may be thinking...Why should I trust this and will it actually work for me and my teen? As a parent you are probably feeling extremely frustrated. Having a teen is nothing like it is in the movies and we (teens) feel the same way on the other side. I can tell you from personal experience that the things you will learn reading this book will work to connect you with your son or daughter and have many "talks" on difficult topics!

As the daughter of Dr. Jennifer Salerno, I have lived through the examples and strategies you will read about throughout this book. As a young adult now, I can look back and tell you that being a teen is hard! As a teen, there are a million things going on in your head all at once and you are trying to figure out what all of these new thoughts and emotions mean. You compare yourself to others around you, your friends are talking about trying drugs and alcohol, they are having sex, social media is capturing everything you do for everyone to see and comment on...you have to figure out how all of this fits with how YOU see yourself. In the midst of all of this we are looking for someone to talk to that understands us and will listen, and who already went through it all.

As a teen, I definitely did not make parenting easy for my mom and dad. When I was an early teen I liked to eat a lot of unhealthy food, I liked to fight with my Dad, and I was 'always right'. As you can imagine I needed my parents to use the strategies in this book in order to save our relationship and for us to be able to have conversations that weren't always arguments. Thankfully, my mom was constantly empowering me to make positive decisions and to help me stay on track with the goals that I had for myself.

On top of all the good advice and positive conversations with my mom, my family made it a priority to have dinners together. This is what I attribute everything to when it comes to how close and comfortable I am with talking about really anything with my mom, dad and younger brother. Our dinner conversations ranged anywhere from talking about our grades and futures, to sexually transmitted diseases, and what it means to be drunk or high. None of the conversations were forced and it all came naturally...when we were able to unplug and spend time on nothing but eating (a healthy meal of course) and talking with each other.

Along with family dinners, car rides (even just to the grocery store) were great times that I got to vent about my day and talk about things with my family. In a car you are almost 'trapped' into conversation because you are in such a small area with parents who are asking about you and your life. To this day I still look forward to the conversations we have on longer car rides when I get to sit in the front seat with my mom or dad.

All and all, my advice: use this book, love this book. I know this sounds cheesy, but from my experiences living with parents who use these strategies I have formed a relationship with my mom and dad that outshines the best ones you see in the movies and TV!

Good Luck!

Jordyn

■ ■ ■

Introduction

The Birth of *Teen Speak*

I absolutely love teens! I know that sounds crazy - but I couldn't wait for my own kids to become teenagers. While the transition to the teen years can bring many normal feelings of concern and worry – it can be an enjoyable, exciting time as well.

As a nurse practitioner, a researcher, and a mom of two, I am writing this book with the hope that it will help you feel more prepared to support your teenager through their extreme ups and downs – and at the same time create and maintain a strong, positive relationship that your teen can lean on throughout this time of dramatic change in their lives.

Over the years, I have counseled thousands of teens on their risky behaviors. When I use the phrase **risky behaviors** throughout this book, I mean it to encompass all issues that put teens at greater risk of harm. Behaviors like drug and alcohol use and sex; experiences of being bullied or abused; and feelings of anxiety or depression. My reference to risky behaviors describes something a teen is choosing to do, has experienced, or is feeling.

What I have learned, in both my professional work with teens and when talking with my son's and daughter's friends, is that most teens have never been directly asked about their behaviors. As a professional, whenever I identified risky behaviors in my teen patients, I would ask who they had talked with besides me. The most common reply was "*No one has ever asked, so I have never talked about it.*" Some teens did say that their parents told them not to do something like drink or have sex, but for most teens, their parents never had a real talk with them asking deeper questions like what their thoughts were about specific risky behaviors, if they had engaged in them, and how they planned to keep themselves safe.

Parents tend to rely on healthcare providers to ask the *right* questions and give information to their teens, at least for those teens getting regular check-ups. This may seem like a good strategy because it can be hard for many teens to talk honestly with their parents and for parents to feel comfortable with topics that may be on their teen's mind.

The problem with that strategy lies with the fact that many healthcare providers are also uncomfortable talking with teens about their risky behaviors and do not ask questions and give information in a way that invites teens to share and have open discussions with them. It is very common for healthcare providers to ask questions like, "*You're not having sex, right?*" or "*You aren't drinking or smoking, are you?*" This gives the teen an out to avoid sharing honestly what they are doing (or thinking about doing). Often, their response is a shake of their head with an automatic "*nope*" and nothing further gets discussed.

Don't feel discouraged by this. There are healthcare providers out there who are able to connect with teens. My intention in raising this issue is to point out that even trained professionals may have difficulties communicating with teens. As a parent you should be aware of the quality of care that is being provided to your son or daughter. That is why it is so important for you to know *how* to talk with teens about their risky behaviors – if parents and professionals aren't doing it, who is?

You can have real talks with your teen! **There are lots of ways of talking with teens that help them feel more comfortable sharing honest information about their behaviors. There are also many strategies that encourage them to consider options for making safer, more positive decisions.** By talking about risky behaviors **with** teens instead of **at** them, I have witnessed teens make safer decisions about using substances and having sex, work to overcome depression and anxiety, and ask for help when they were being bullied or experiencing violence.

Witnessing these positive changes in the teens I worked with was so exciting, that I wanted to help all healthcare providers feel more comfortable and learn how to talk *with* their teen patients about risky behaviors instead of the usual approach of telling them what to do. I began by creating a training for healthcare providers.

The training focuses on how to identify and talk with teens about their behaviors in a way that encourages and supports them in making safer, more positive decisions. As I trained professionals around the country, the message I kept hearing from them was how they wished they would have had this training when their own children were teenagers. Armed with this information, those teen years would have been a lot less stressful. I also heard from health professionals who had teenagers at the time they were in the training. They shared stories about how the training helped them change the way they were talking with their own teens and that their relationships were getting stronger.

One participant said her daughter told her, *"Finally, you get it!"* At the same time, outside of my professional trainings, I was being asked by friends and family members with teens to share my "secrets" with them.

So from one parent to another – here are my thoughts, knowledge and experiences. I hope that you will find strategies that work for you and your teen to open the door to the very important (and ongoing) discussion on risky behaviors!

Congratulations – You Are the Parent of a Teenager!

Half of your son's or daughter's childhood is spent as a pre-teen (tween) or teenager – yet as a parent, you don't receive much guidance in understanding or supporting them. Becoming the parent of a teenager is scary! Who needs concrete, actionable advice more than the parent of a teenager? Unfortunately, our healthcare system often fails to support us in one of the most critical aspects of parenting: understanding and supporting our sons and daughters during their teen years and beyond, to guide them onto becoming successful young adults.

There is no formal preparation like the prenatal classes you took before they were born. No one is there to congratulate you, share in the excitement of your son's or daughter's growth in height and weight, or in their new abilities in throwing a ball (this time on a sports team). You don't have eight doctor visits scheduled in the first two years of adolescence, like the time between your child's birth and when they turned two years old.

Unless your teen plays sports, your son or daughter may not have gotten a physical examination (check-up) from their health care provider in several years. If they have had a check-up, it is even less likely that any time was spent giving you tips such as what to expect as your teen grows, support for the demands of being a parent of a teenager, or guidance on how to encourage independence yet ensure your son or daughter isn't taking too many risks. Advice from well-meaning friends and family is often contradictory or just plain unhelpful: "*Just get through it…they will be better once they are out of your house…there isn't much you can do at this age.*"

It can feel like you were thrown into parenting a teenager without warning and you're left wondering, "*What did I miss?*" You wake up one day with a mini-teen at 9 years old, and you are thinking, this is WAY TOO SOON! You may remember when your son or daughter started elementary school and you saw the physical differences between the first graders and the fifth graders, but it seemed so far away…and anyway, fifth graders are still kids. It seemed like you still had a long time before you had to worry about more than what the next Disney cartoon would be or how to entice them to play outside. As they grew, you did notice the little changes (changes that may have hit you hard emotionally) – like when they didn't want to hold your hand or give you a hug in public, especially when you dropped them off at school.

The child that clung to you and begged you not to leave them on that first day of school, is now running out of the car with barely a good-bye. Friends are now their priority. Clothes are changed several times every morning, many times with tears flowing or anger exploding over how they look. And this is just the beginning…

The teen years are SO IMPORTANT in helping your son or daughter become successful young adults. Through this book, I am sharing information and tools you can use to create a relationship with your teen that supports **real talks** and discussions. Talks that don't include explosions (from you or your teen), ignoring (when teens are focusing on their phone instead of you), or *yessing* you to death (telling you, "*Sure, I got it,*" to end the conversation and leave the room).

Every parent's dream is to talk with their teen, to feel like they are really being heard and their advice is being used by their teen to make better decisions. Let's get closer to making that dream a reality!

■ ■ ■

Before You Get Started

This book was written for parents looking to strengthen their relationship with their son or daughter – whether you are preparing for your child's teenage years or you already have a teenager. My hope is that this book will help you understand the changes our sons and daughters go through as they become teenagers; that you will become more aware of the behaviors that put teens at risk; and to give you some new and different ways to talk with your teen about risky behaviors.

Ultimately my goal is for you to use the communication strategies included in this book to positively influence your son's or daughter's decisions about things like texting and driving, using substances, and sex. This is not a book on how to parent your teenager. However, the strategies can be used when talking with your son or daughter about many different situations that will come up over the course of their teen years, not just with talks about risky behaviors.

As a parent you do have some control over what your teen is or is not doing based on your household rules, and the rewards and punishments you have decided to enforce when those rules are broken. Many teens will do one thing and tell you they are doing something else – as you know, they are very clever at finding ways to get away with something you have told them not to do.

Over the years I have talked with many teens both professionally and with my own son's and daughter's friends. On one side, I hear parents saying things like, *"My son has never had a sip of alcohol; we lock up everything in the house,"* or, *"My daughter is waiting until she is married to have sex,"* and on the other side, I know that these same teens are the ones getting drunk at parties on the weekends and having casual sex.

That is scary to think about as a parent. We love and want to protect our sons and daughters, and part of that protection is telling them what to do and not to do and creating consequences if they decide to break these rules. It is our job as parents, right? Definitely - we create rules and boundaries for our sons and daughters to keep them safe. The strategies I will share throughout this book may at times seem counterintuitive to this idea. Keep in mind that I'm not saying we shouldn't parent our teens, rather I'm suggesting the way that we talk with our teens about our expectations and their behaviors will make a big difference in what they decide to do when they are out of our sight.

Incorporating the strategies in this book will help you create a relationship between you and your teen that will support real discussions around risky behaviors – particularly those behaviors that forced you to create household rules and punishments in the first place. When you have real discussions **with** your teen and are not just talking *at* or *to* your teen, they are more likely to follow your rules when they are faced with risky situations.

You need to know that using the strategies described in this book takes PRACTICE and PATIENCE. It is not a one time, try it and done approach. As much as I'd like to say that it's easy – it just isn't. You will have to continue to practice and find the strategies that work best to support conversations between you and your teen.

Practicing and trying out the strategies in this book can help you learn what your teen responds to best (different strategies work with different teens). Also keep in mind that some strategies will work better in certain situations than in others. It takes time to consistently apply the strategies and build a relationship with your teen that supports **real** discussions. The fact that you are taking the time to read this book shows your commitment to establishing a strong, positive relationship with your son or daughter during their teen years and beyond!

Throughout this book I'm going to give you common situations and alternative ways of talking with your teen about risky behaviors or difficult topics. I start by giving examples right away, but we don't get into the details of each of the strategies and how to use them until Section 2. Don't let that overwhelm or discourage you. Read through the examples as a way to better understand what putting these strategies into place looks and sounds like.

Once you finish Section 2, go back and read through the examples provided in Section 1 again. You will have a new perspective on how and why each strategy was used. By doing this, you get more comfortable with these new strategies of talking with your teen. Another way to get comfortable with the strategies is to read this book with your partner or friends and practice the strategies with each other. The fastest way to learn something new is by having another person supporting and learning with you.

Share the experiences you are having when talking with your teen (you probably do this already). Ask for advice from your partner or friend by sharing what strategies you used that may not have worked so well and learn about the different strategies they have used successfully that you might want to try. By doing this, you will create your own parent support group and now instead of complaining about your teens (we have all been there), you can focus on building strong, positive relationships with them!

■ ■ ■

Section 1

Getting to Know Your Teen

1

Foundations For Talking *With* Your Teen

I have spent my entire career, over 20 years as a nurse practitioner, working with teens. All were intelligent, beautiful young people with endless possibilities ahead of them. When thinking about all of the teens I have worked with, the biggest differences in their success or failure came in their decisions around risky behaviors — and how the consequences of unhealthy decisions darkened their futures.

Most people don't know the unmentionable truth: that the causes of death in 3 out of every 4 teens are due to their risky behaviors (texting and driving, drinking alcohol, suicide). These statistics are published every year by the U.S. Centers for Disease Control and Prevention, yet the media and the healthcare system turn a blind eye because there is no easy answer, no pill to prescribe to improve these statistics. These are deaths that could have been prevented if a parent was aware, if a healthcare provider was aware AND the teen had conversations with caring adults in ways that caused them to think differently about risks and then actually make safer decisions.

This is where it gets tough. This is where both parents and healthcare providers often throw in the towel — before they even ask the first question. Because honestly, it is much more comfortable when we *don't ask* and they *don't tell*.

Continuing with the painful truth, it is difficult to hear answers like these from your teen:

- *Yes, I'm having sex.*
- *Yes, I'm texting and driving.*
- *Yes, I'm drinking with my friends.*
- *Yes, these feelings of sadness are getting worse and I feel like I want to die.*

This type of truth produces a strong (natural) reaction of protection and a tremendous amount of anxiety and stress over what we should do next. We know the possible consequences of these "*yes*" answers because we have lived through some of them ourselves...stop and take a deep breath!

At this point, if we have gotten teens to tell us the truth about their behaviors (which is actually a huge win in and of itself) our initial physical response causes a fight or flight reaction. As parents, even though we desperately want flight, (to run away and pretend we didn't hear them say *that*) – the fight response usually wins. We start to tell our son or daughter why their behavior doesn't make sense. "*Don't you know what can happen when you drink* (insert "bad" things that happen)? *I don't want you to ever see* (insert name) *again,*" and it often ends with an "*or else.*"

After this lecture, you may also throw in a story of when you were a teen and dealt with these same issues....blah, blah, blah. Your teen listens half-heartedly (regretting the fact that they told you about drinking and promising themselves they won't tell you next time), agrees (having no real plan to actually stop the behavior), and then figures out a better way to hide it from you.

The way we are talking with teens is simply not working. Even though the risk behaviors have changed over the years (texting and sexting for example) the statistics have not changed much in over 30 years: 3 out of 4 teen deaths are still related to preventable risky behaviors.

Before we continue, if something terrible has happened to your teen or a teen you know, I am so sorry! I am not saying that you are responsible for their decisions and the unfortunate consequences. As much as we would like to be able to monitor everything that our kids do and be there to stop them from making what we would consider bad decisions, it just isn't possible.

I am suggesting that there are ways to talk with your teen that may work better and that may help them *hear* what you are saying and make decisions that are safer and healthier for them. **Studies show that having a strong relationship with your teen is one of the biggest positive influences on their behaviors.**

There are ways to talk with teens that have been researched and shown to work better than lecturing and telling them what to do. Using these strategies as a parent feels weird at first. We are the parent and our kids should listen and do whatever we tell them to do. While I am not disagreeing with this ideal, it is not reality for most teens. Parenting is a balance between respecting our teens by allowing them to make decisions that they can learn from – and directing their lives by giving them rules and guidelines to live by.

Take a few minutes to think about when you were a teen...

- How did your parents talk to you about risky behaviors?
- How did that make you feel?
- Did you listen and do exactly as they said?

■ ■ ■

Think about risky behaviors as a continuum — some behaviors are lower risk and some are higher risk. In the following example of alcohol use, think about the level of risk (low-high):

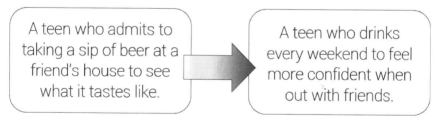

A teen who admits to taking a sip of beer at a friend's house to see what it tastes like.

A teen who drinks every weekend to feel more confident when out with friends.

Risk taking is a part of normal teen development. It is the type and level of risk that should cause us to be concerned. Even low risk in some behaviors can have serious consequences. I am hoping this book will increase your understanding of teens and their behaviors and how to talk with them, ultimately strengthening your relationship with your son or daughter, so that when they are faced with choices about participating in risky behaviors, they will make safer decisions.

You will learn ways to talk with teens that will set the stage for honest conversations about behaviors – particularly behaviors that may lead to serious injury or death. These are conversations that will support your teen in making safer decisions – conversations that will save lives and help move the needle on our statistics in a positive direction!

Before we jump into the different ways to talk with teens, I would like to start by discussing the big changes happening in your teen's body and mind that are affecting their feelings and emotions, and ultimately influencing their decisions. These changes are the primary causes of your son's or daughter's moods, angry outbursts, tears, indecisiveness, and the many other *out-there* behaviors you are seeing.

All of these big changes make it difficult for you and your teen to have a positive relationship. When you understand these changes and sympathize with your teen rather than get frustrated or angry with them (our normal reactions), your relationship and communication will improve.

Setting the stage for talking with your teen starts by knowing some important information about:

- What is happening inside their bodies as they grow from being children to teens to young adults,

- What kinds of risky behaviors are most common during this time in their lives, and

- What strengths teens have that they could use to help them make safer decisions.

Having this background and understanding will set the stage for learning new ways to talk with the teens in your life!

■ ■ ■

Chapter 1 – Take Home Messages

✓ The causes of death in 3 out of every 4 teens are due to their risky behaviors. The good news is that these are deaths that have the potential to be prevented by parents engaging in ongoing talks *with* their teens – talks that cause teens to think differently about risky situations and make safer decisions.

✓ Now is the time to develop a strong, supportive relationship with your teen – no matter what their age. Studies show that having a strong relationship with your teen is one of the biggest positive influences on their behaviors.

✓ There are ways to talk with teens that have been studied and shown to work better than lecturing and telling them what to do. You are on your way to learning and practicing these new strategies to support *real* conversations around risky behaviors!

2

Teen Development –
The Good, the Bad and the Beautiful

What to expect – when you are parenting a teenager! The biggest thing to remember when you are frustrated with how your son or daughter is behaving is that they have no control over the changes happening in their bodies. They are riding a roller-coaster of highs and lows.

Think about what it is like to go through menopause and middle age (or what you've heard about it), multiply that by 100 and put yourself in an environment where all of your friends and co-workers are going through the same thing. Sounds horrible, right? That is what our teens are dealing with every day.

The process of extreme growth and change starts around nine years old and goes all the way through twenty-one. The biggest changes happen between the ages of thirteen and seventeen. These years are called **adolescence** or are referred to as the **adolescent years**, although you may also hear these years referred to as **puberty**.

At no other time (except in their first two years of life) do our sons and daughters go through so much change, so quickly. Understanding exactly what is happening (and why it is happening) can help you support your son or daughter during this physically and emotionally challenging time. It may also help to lessen some of the frustration you are feeling toward them.

Studies suggest there are three primary stages of development teens go through as they are changing from children into young adults. The stages are called:

- Early Adolescence
- Middle Adolescence
- Late Adolescence

The ages for each stage overlap and vary based on gender.

| EARLY ADOLESCENCE | MIDDLE ADOLESCENCE | LATE ADOLESCENCE |
| 11 – 14 YEARS | 14 – 17 YEARS | 17 – 21 YEARS |

| EARLY ADOLESCENCE | MIDDLE ADOLESCENCE | LATE ADOLESCENCE |
| 9 – 13 YEARS | 13 – 16 YEARS | 16 – 21 YEARS |

It is important to note that these age ranges are just guidelines. Not all teens will develop neatly along this path and you may see many differences in your own teen's development. The information provided in this book is meant as a guide.

Unfortunately, these stages were created using studies that looked mostly at white, middle-class teens. There is a gap in research on normal development for all teens. This may be something to keep in mind if your teen doesn't fit this category as you read on about development.

Within each of these stages of development (early, middle and late), teens experience many changes – and these changes are categorized into:

- Physical (affecting the body)
- Cognitive (thinking and brain development)
- Emotional (impacting their feelings)
- Sexual

Teens develop within each of these categories (physically, cognitively, emotionally, and sexually) at different rates, and this uneven development is normal and healthy.

While your son or daughter may develop physically by middle adolescence, their cognitive and emotional development may still need to catch up. Everyone has known, or knows, a teen that physically looks like an adult but emotionally and cognitively still acts like a child. This can be very frustrating as you, or other adults, expect more mature thinking and control over emotions from teens that look like adults on the outside than from teens who do not.

Early development in one area (having the body of an adult) doesn't mean that a teen is equally developed in all areas (being able to think and reason like an adult). Development in each area is a gradual process with stops and starts. Growth spurts will occur in different areas of development (like physical growth and emotional growth) at different times. Sometimes just keeping this front of mind and taking a deep breath before having difficult talks can help you be more patient!

■ ■ ■

Chapter 2 – Take Home Messages

✓ At no other time (except in their first two years of life) do our sons and daughters go through so much growth and change, so quickly.

✓ Growth spurts will occur in different areas of development (like physical growth and emotional growth) at different times. While your son or daughter may develop physically by middle adolescence, their cognitive and emotional development may still need to catch up.

✓ Understanding exactly what is happening (and why it is happening) during adolescence can help you support your son or daughter during this physically and emotionally challenging time.

3

Physical Development – Body Changes

Teens experience a tremendous amount of physical growth during adolescence. It is really important during this time that your teen is eating healthy foods that will support their growth and development. Growth in height during adolescence averages **8 inches**.

In addition to significant changes in height, teens also experience changes in their body's ratio of fat to lean muscle mass. A teen boy's lean muscle mass greatly increases due to the rising levels of hormones like testosterone. Teen girls continue to develop muscle mass while also adding body fat. During adolescence, girls' percentage of body fat will increase. This additional fat is deposited in the midsection (hips, buttocks, and chest) and can be upsetting for some girls. Increase in weight during adolescence for both girls and boys averages **45 pounds**.

These physical changes can affect a teen's self-image, mood, and relationships – both positively and negatively. The timing of physical development can affect a teen's emotional development in many ways. Because teens who physically mature earlier appear older, they're often treated as if they are more socially and emotionally mature, even though this often isn't true.

Boys and girls whose bodies develop earlier than their friends and classmates are more likely to engage in risky behaviors at earlier ages. These early developing teens may start hanging out with or dating older teens who expose them to situations like sex and alcohol before they are developmentally ready to handle it.

Younger teens are more likely to "go with the flow" and engage in the behaviors just to fit in with their older peers.

 Things to watch out for as your son or daughter develops physically:

- Fear and withdrawal (especially in early adolescence).
- An obsessive concern about their appearance – causing them to miss school or events because they *"didn't look right."*
- Excessive dieting or exercise – which can quickly lead to eating disorders.
- Being bullied, teased, or excluded by friends or other teens.

» What you can do...

Don't blow off comments your son or daughter is making about their body. Take these comments seriously and spend time **listening** (without jumping in and talking). Sometimes growth spurts cause clothes to fit more tightly and look different. Make sure the clothes your teen is wearing are the right size and style for their body type. They will change sizes quickly during early and middle adolescence. Encourage your son or daughter to explore their feelings and to pinpoint what is stressing them out about their bodies.

During growth spurts, you may experience something like this in your home:

You hear screaming and something hit your daughter's bedroom door. You notice her jeans on the floor and realize she was trying to put on jeans that she has outgrown.

- Start by acknowledging her feelings, "*You are upset about not fitting into your favorite jeans.*"
- Allow her to respond, "*Yes, I'm so fat right now! I hate myself!*"
- Follow-up with understanding and information: "*You are going through a hard time right now. Your body is growing really fast and your clothes can't grow with it.*"
- Pause to allow your daughter to respond, "*I wish I would just stop growing.*"
- You respond with a different view of the situation and a possible solution: "*Changing sizes is a normal part of getting older. What if we go out this weekend and buy you a few things to fit the 'new you'?*"

You will be tempted to tell them things like, "*You don't have to look like everyone else. You are perfect just as you are. The people you see on TV and in magazines aren't normal.*" These may be true statements – but not necessarily what they need to hear.

Try something like this next time:

- Your son comes home from school and says, "*I hate being short! I can't do anything!*"
- Start by acknowledging what you heard him say that may help to pinpoint the underlying issue: "*You are feeling left out*" (try not to focus on what he can't control – which is his height).
- Allow him to respond, "*Yeah, I'm so short I'll never make the basketball team.*"
- Follow-up with something like, "*You are missing out on time with your friends by not being part of the team.*"
- Pause for a response, "*Yeah, I never see them anymore. They are always too busy!*"
- Help him start to problem solve the issue: "*Hanging out with your friends is important. What do you think about inviting them over on a Saturday? That way it won't interfere with their practice time.*"

If your son's or daughter's body develops early, encourage them to continue friendships with girls and boys their own age and to not start hanging out with an older crowd.

If you suspect an eating disorder or your son or daughter is not coping well with the physical changes happening in their bodies, seek help and support from a counselor. If you don't know a counselor in your area, your health care provider or your teen's school counselor may be able to help connect you with someone.

■ ■ ■

Chapter 3 - Understanding Physical Development

Early Adolescence Girls 9-13 years Boys 11-14 years	Middle Adolescence Girls 13-16 years Boys 14-17 years	Late Adolescence Girls 16-21 years Boys 17-21 years
• Extreme growth of height and weight lasting 2-4 years • Increased appetite • Increase in hormones • Menstrual periods begin for many girls • Hips widen in girls • Breasts enlarge and can be sore in girls • Testicles and penis enlarge in boys • Pubic hair appears • Hands and feet grow faster, followed by arms and legs, affecting coordination • Body odor and acne begins • Voices get deeper for boys	• Full physical development continues to the end of this stage • 95% of adult height is reached • Breast, testicle and penis growth continues • Underarm hair appears; facial and body hair for boys • Continued growth leads to waves of increased appetite and physical activity, followed by lethargy and decreased appetite	• Physical growth leveling off and ending

4

Cognitive Development – Thinking Skills

Changes in how teens think, reason, and understand can be even more dramatic than the physical changes you can see.

During adolescence, teens:

- Strengthen their advanced reasoning skills (skills used to think about multiple options and possibilities for a given situation). This includes the ability to think through various "*What if...?*" scenarios for different situations.

- Develop abstract thinking skills (skills used to think about things that can't be seen, heard or touched – like love or beliefs).

- Develop meta-cognition, which is literally thinking about thinking (skills used to think about how they feel about a situation, and how they are viewed by others).

It is normal for teens to be very black and white (or concrete) thinkers one day, and then seemingly overnight they are able to think more broadly and in shades of grey. When this happens, celebrate your teen's cognitive development! While their cognitive abilities can appear to progress rapidly, **teens don't use their new abilities consistently** over time or apply them evenly across situations.

When talking with teens about risky behaviors, their level of cognitive development will determine their ability to think about different options for lowering their risk for a particular behavior.

- If a teen is feeling depressed, the more developed they are in their cognitive skills (thinking), the more they may:
  - Consider options for improving their mood like journaling, listening to music, exercising, joining a club or sport at school, or talking with a counselor.
  - Think about how they feel about the people closest to them and choose to only hang out with friends who make them feel good about themselves.
  - Think more deeply about a situation to determine the times when they feel most depressed and when they feel the most happy and make decisions about what they are going to do based on what makes them feel the best.

As teens mature, their decision making skills increase, but in stressful situations they often revert back to the concrete thinking of early development. There are very distinct individual differences in cognitive development among teens. When they reach late cognitive development they are able to consistently reason, problem solve, think abstractly, and plan for their future.

■ ■ ■

Cognitive development in teens can be very frustrating.

Here are a few key points to remember as your son's or daughter's cognitive skills are developing:

It's normal for teens to...

Argue for the sake of arguing: New reasoning skills can feel exciting to teens and they will take opportunities to try them out with you, which won't feel as exciting for you. You will notice that your son or daughter has begun arguing with you about everything – even things you think don't matter. Keep in mind, this is a part of their development. Try not to engage in a tug-of-war with them every time they have a different viewpoint.

- Start by listening to their point of view. Choose your battles by thinking to yourself: **Is this worth arguing about or can I let it go?** You could easily find yourself arguing with your teen every time you are together. Find a happy medium.

- Build trust by encouraging healthy debate. Set ground rules by taking the time to create guidelines for how you will talk and how you will listen to each other. The guidelines should be agreed upon and used by both you and your teen, especially during heated talks.

  - Start the conversation about ground rules by sharing your thoughts and feelings: *"We have been arguing a lot lately and I don't want that to affect our relationship. I would like us to set some 'rules' to follow whenever we start disagreeing about something. Are you OK with this?"*

  - Next share a rule you would like to have: *"When we are disagreeing about something, I would like us to take turns sharing our thoughts one at a time. When one person is talking, the other person listens. That way we are not trying to talk over each other or to talk louder than the other person."*

  - Ask your teen to come up with some rules too: *"What else do you think we could do to make sure our disagreements don't get out of control?"*

- The key to managing arguing behavior in your teen is to keep *your* emotions in control. It can feel very disrespectful to have your son or daughter argue against something you want them to do, to make sarcastic comments, or raise their voice to you.

Take a deep breath. Your teen is also feeling disrespected by you (right or wrong). Have an open conversation about what respect looks and feels like. *"I am feeling really disrespected by you right now and I know you are probably feeling disrespected too."* A simple statement like this during a heated argument can be very powerful in bringing the emotions down in order to be able to discuss the real issue in a calmer, more productive way.

If you have a spouse, partner or another adult who is parenting with you, you may want to decide who is better able to stay calm and have that person talk with your teen about issues that you know are going to cause them to become angry or could escalate quickly.

Jump to conclusions: Teens have difficulty thinking through a situation, considering all of their possible options, and understanding how others feel about it. As their cognitive skills develop, they improve in these areas. Lots of times teens jump to conclusions (as many adults do, too) without considering the alternatives.

- Try not to correct every faulty logic point your son or daughter is trying to make. Ask them how they arrived at a particular thought or conclusion instead of arguing with them about it.

  □ When your son comes home from school and says he is not doing well in math because the teacher hates him, you might ask something like, *"What makes you think your teacher hates you,"* instead of responding with an immediate (normal) reaction of, *"No she doesn't. Maybe you aren't studying enough or doing your homework if you are failing math."*

- Never make fun of their thoughts or ideas, especially in front of other people. A statement like, *"That is ridiculous,"* when they share something with you can feel devastating to a teen – and can cause them to not share things in the future.

- Encourage a deeper understanding of the things your teen shares by directing them to accurate, factual information. For important topics (particularly behaviors that could affect your teen's life), take a few minutes to research background information – the internet is a fast and easy way to do this.

  □ For example, if your teen says, *"We talked about texting and driving in health class today, but they were just trying to scare us."*

  □ Search the internet to find out how many teens in your city or state got in accidents last year because of texting and driving. Starting a discussion with these facts can be much more powerful then launching into a lecture about why texting and driving is dangerous. Specific information that hits home in some way can help to give your teen a deeper understanding of the seriousness of the issue. The more relevant you can make it to their lives, the more powerful it will be.

Be self-centered: A part of normal teen development is the sense that the world revolves around them. This self-centeredness stems from brain changes causing teens to think more deeply about their identity – how they feel about themselves, and how others view them. They can be very self-absorbed during the process. At the same time teens are becoming more aware of, and interested in, issues that are bigger than themselves. Concern for others and for societal issues emerges in late adolescence.

- Cognitive skills can be sharpened by encouraging teens to talk about their views – whether those are political, spiritual, or views on world events. Be ready for some of their views to be the complete opposite of yours. Be sure you don't make fun of, ignore or diminish their views; instead, encourage them to find out more about the stand that they are taking.

    ◦ Often teens feel strongly about a particular issue and make changes in their behaviors to support their views. An example is a teen who decides to become a vegetarian after hearing a story about animals that are raised for food.

- Help your teen consider someone else's thoughts or feelings by making matter of fact statements (while being aware of your body language and tone of voice) that provide another person's point of view. For example, "*Even though he didn't show it, your brother was really hurt when you told him he would never get a prom date.*"

Constantly find fault in your position: Teens' newfound abilities to think critically causes them to look for flaws or inconsistencies in what adults say. This happens most when teens feel safe with you and comfortable enough to share their views honestly. Little did you know, it is a compliment to your relationship when teens point out flaws in what you are saying.

- Try not to take it personally and get into an argument. Explain your point of view and clarify any mix-ups.

- Limit sharing personal experiences when clarifying your position on something. "*I'm telling you this because when I was 16...*" Teens don't respond well when you share stories about your own experiences. This is hard for parents to understand – especially when we have experiences that we feel will help our teens make better decisions!

Do you remember a time from your teen years when your parent shared a personal story about something (maybe a near pregnancy or car accident) and it made a difference in how you felt about a situation? It is very unlikely that you responded "*yes*" to this question. Teens disregard our stories, bottom line. When we share our personal stories, it can make teens feel like they are not being heard and that their experiences are being dismissed. This typically results in them being angry or withdrawing from the conversation.

- If you must share your personal story, listen first to everything your son or daughter has to share with you – try not to interrupt. Ask some probing questions about their feelings **before** you share your own experiences. You might ask something simple like, "*How does that make you feel?*"

- When you do share a personal story, keep it short and simple.

 **Be overly dramatic:** Hormones during adolescence, and the emotions that come with those hormones, can make everything seem like a big deal to teens. They have very little (if any) control over the assault of emotions they are feeling throughout the day. One minute they will be on top of the world and the next they will feel like the sky is falling.

This is one of the most difficult parts of parenting a teen. You never know what their mood will be from one minute to the next. Just like when they were babies and you weren't sure when they would start crying – or if you were going to be able to get them to stop, it can be very anxiety provoking and cause a lot of stress in your home. My husband would often ask me, "*What is the def-con level today?*" as he was coming home from work. He liked to prepare himself for the emotional roller coaster.

Help teens think through their dramatic or exaggerated response by reflecting their *drama* and asking open-ended, clarifying questions.

You may encounter a situation like this:

- Your teen says, "*Jessie broke up with me, I can never show my face at school again.*"
  - You might respond with something like, "*You will have to drop out of school and get a GED.*" The drama is reflected back to your son or daughter in a neutral (matter of fact) statement – be very careful of your body language and tone of voice. This is not meant to be sarcastic.

- Allow your teen to respond to your statement – typically they will back off of the exaggeration.
- Follow up with a question like, *"What would it take for you to feel OK going to school tomorrow?"* and brainstorm ideas with your son or daughter.
- If they respond *"nothing"* to your question, help them see the situation differently. *"We both know you have to go to school. I care about you and want to help you figure out what would make it easier."*

- You may need to give them some time to calm down before you can have a conversation. Ask them, *"I want to talk to you about* [insert situation]. *Can we do that right now? If not, how much time do you need?"*

- Strong feelings like anger, sadness or excitement can overshadow the truth of a situation. Encourage teens to **sleep on it** if they have strong feelings about something to be sure their decisions are not being clouded by emotion.

■ ■ ■

》 What you can do...

For all of these *normal teen behaviors*, the way you respond can help your son or daughter develop positive decision making and coping skills. The more you stay calm, be directive in your conversations, and role model good communication, the more likely your teen will be able to navigate their changing thoughts and emotions to develop into successful young adults.

■ ■ ■

Early Adolescence Girls 9-13 years Boys 11-14 years	**Middle Adolescence** Girls 13-16 years Boys 14-17 years	**Late Adolescence** Girls 16-21 years Boys 17-21 years
• Concrete thinking – focus is on the present "here and now" • Limited understanding of the cause and effect in situations • Thoughts of the future are limited • Improved ability to use speech to express themselves, but more likely to express their feelings by actions (like punching a wall when they are angry)	• Abstract thinking – can think about the future • Concrete thinking reemerges in times of stress • Self-absorbed • Denial of the consequences of their behaviors • Future oriented – ability to set goals • Importance is placed on setting long-term goals and their ability to follow through with them increases • Development of ideals and selection of role models	• Ability to think ideas through and make independent decisions • Can consider multiple points of view and multiple "right" answers to problems • Feelings are expressed using words • Concern for the future and thoughts of their own role in life • Concern for others and for societal issues

5

Emotional Development – Feelings

A teen's physical and cognitive development influences their emotional development (how they feel about something or someone). As cognitive (thinking) skills deepen, teens begin to create an image of themselves (an identity). Physical changes they are experiencing strongly influence (good or bad) their identity and self-esteem. This is especially true in early adolescence. Identity formation is an ongoing process as teens build cognitive skills to sort through who they are and what makes them different.

A teen's emotional development includes figuring out how to deal with:

- Friends
- Dating
- Family
- School
- Community
- Work

One of the most significant changes in emotional development in teens (and most difficult for parents to handle) is the shift from the world revolving around family to revolving around friends.

Emotional development includes **self-awareness, social awareness, self-management,** and the **ability to get along with others and make friends.**

- **Self-awareness** centers on teens learning to recognize and name their feelings. Feelings can't be named unless teens are first aware of them, and second are able to think about them (this is a part of cognitive development). Without this awareness, un-named feelings can become uncomfortable enough that teens become withdrawn, depressed, angry, or turn to substances to feel better.

- **Social awareness** is the awareness of what other people are feeling, along with developing compassion, taking into account the feelings of others, and appreciating the value of human differences.

- **Self-management** means teens are learning to control their emotions and are capable of establishing and working toward positive goals. Self-management increases with the increase in testosterone (hormone) in both boys and girls, affecting the areas of the brain that cause them to have strong responses to feelings that go along with particular behaviors (like sex) and particular emotions (like love).

- Finally, emotional development depends on **establishing healthy, rewarding relationships.** As part of their identity formation, teens explore and "try on" a variety of different roles, personalities, ways of behaving, beliefs, interests, and values.

Key emotional development indicators in teens include:

- Becoming more independent
- Developing close relationships with people outside of their families
- Developing an increased need and capacity for intimacy (feeling close to another person)

Peer pressure during adolescence is something parents often worry about. In early and middle adolescence, teens are particularly vulnerable to peer pressure and in general boys are more vulnerable to peer pressure than girls. However, while friends have a big influence on teens' day-to-day identity choices (like clothing or music), research shows that **having family members who teens feel connected to is even more important** during adolescence than at any other time. A family that a teen feels connected to has a **powerful effect** on that teen's basic values and decisions.

Don't disconnect with your teen during their adolescent years. This is a critical time to make sure you stay connected! Keep talking…eat family dinners together…plan outings for just you and your teen (an offer of shopping is hard for teens to resist)…plan a weekend get-away (no friends or extended family invited). **Adolescence is an important time to solidify your relationship with your teen.** Remind your son or daughter of the important role they play in your family.

Some of the best conversations I have had with my own teens about risky behaviors have been after we have settled in somewhere for the weekend, at dinner (when no one is rushed to get somewhere), on longer drives (my husband sits in the backseat with one of our kids and the other one sits up front with me), or while watching a teen TV show with them. Create expectations for family time with no distractions – liking putting cell phones in another room during dinner (both parents and teens).

 Things to watch out for as your son or daughter develops emotionally:

- Too much focus or concern about their bodies
- Changes in eating or irregular meal patterns (like skipping breakfast or dieting)
- Losing sleep or trouble sleeping
- Ups and downs of social relationships that never seem to end

■ ■ ■

» What you can do...

Too much focus or concern about their bodies

- Talk to your son or daughter about the changes happening in their bodies. It doesn't have to be a sit down, serious conversation. You may say something like, "*Girls hips get wider as they get older and become women.*" Depending on the personality of your daughter you may follow up with, "*Part of becoming a woman is having curves,*" or "*this is your body's way of getting ready to have babies.*" For your son, you may say something similar based on common concerns: "*Your muscles get bigger as you grow older.*"

Little reminders about physical development help to diffuse an emotional situation and assure them that they are "normal."

■ ■ ■

Changes in eating or irregular meal patterns (like skipping breakfast or dieting)

- It is very common for teens to say they are not hungry in the morning or they don't have time to eat, especially on school days. If this is the case, offer a glass of milk or breakfast drink before they leave for school or pack them an extra snack in their lunch. Many schools allow students to eat snacks in their classroom in the morning. Granola bars or fruit like apples are good snacks to pack for them to eat later in the morning.

- Irregular eating patterns are a part of most teens' lives. Many teens are involved in sports, band, or other after school clubs and activities. This, along with parent work schedules and chauffeuring teens back and forth, makes for chaotic evenings. Try to monitor what your teen is eating and when. Don't make it easy for them to skip meals or eat fast food without you knowing.

Family dinners have been shown to make a huge difference in maintaining a positive influence on your teen's life. Even if it is only on the weekends, having family meals are important to your teen's emotional development. Remember to make a rule of no electronics or TV during dinner.

■ ■ ■

Losing sleep or trouble sleeping

- Normal sleep patterns for teens are different than children or adults. Teens are often sleepy when they first wake up, are tired during the day, and then are awake later at night. This pattern is caused by chemicals in their brains triggering these sleep and awake periods.

Teens are going through a tremendous amount of growth during adolescence and need 9-10 hours of sleep each night to rest and recover for the next day. Remember when they were babies and slept all of the time (if you were lucky that is)? They need this same level of sleep as teens. In addition to the chemicals in their brains causing them to be more alert at night, most teens don't get the sleep they need because of early school start times and staying up late to do homework and other activities.

- You can help your teen get quality sleep by keeping TV and other electronics out of their bedrooms (I know, this is difficult), cutting out caffeine in the evening, and getting them to relax and do things to wind down at least a half hour before they go to bed. In particular, they should stop playing video games or games on their phones or other devices at least 30 minutes before going to bed.

- Allow teens to catch-up their sleep on the weekends. Now you know why they sleep until noon, 1 p.m., or longer on Saturdays. They need to catch-up on all the sleep missed during the week! Weekend catch-up sleep is not as good as actually getting 9 hours of sleep each night during the week, but it is necessary to help them get a good start to the following week.

■ ■ ■

Ups and downs of social relationships that never seem to end

- It is normal for teens to have ups and downs with friends, boyfriends or girlfriends, and any other teens they interact with every day. If a disagreement lasts more than a few days or your son or daughter seems extremely depressed or angry, try talking with them about it in more detail. Use feeling statements like, *"You seem really sad about the fight with Lisa,"* or an open ended, question like, *"Tell me what you think happened with Lisa,"* to start the discussion. Try these strategies instead of a more typical question like, *"What is going on with you and Lisa?"* A small tweak in how you ask a question will make a big difference in getting your teen talking.

If needed, seek help and support from a counselor. If you don't know a counselor in your area, your health care provider or your teen's school counselor may be able to help connect you with someone.

 Signs that teens may be emotionally overloaded include:

- Continued complaints of headaches, stomach aches, muscle pain and excessive tiredness.
- Withdrawal from people and activities.
- Increased anger or irritability.
- Crying a lot.

You can help your teen develop healthy relationships by:

- Talking with your son or daughter about what true friendship means. Discuss the differences between good friends and casual friends. Ask *"What would a really good friend be like?"* Be sure to have them focus on inner qualities, common interests, shared activities and quality of interaction. As your teen gets older, they will have the ability to think more deeply about what it means to have a true friend and if any of their current friends have those qualities.

- Helping your son or daughter get involved in things they like or care about. Strong relationships can be formed around mutual interests.

- Talking about boundaries in friendships and romantic relationships. Discuss the importance of establishing limits and respecting alone time. You might start by making a statement, *"I noticed that you are with Aaron all of the time now. You never make plans with anyone else,"* (remember to speak matter-of-factly, without emphasis or judgmental tone).

- Listen to their response and follow it up with a question, *"How do you feel not having time to hang out with your other friends or time for yourself?"* If your son or daughter is in middle or late adolescence you might ask a question to help them to view their situation from another lens: *"What would you say to a friend that was spending all of their time with one person and not hanging out with you anymore?"*

Early Adolescence Girls 9-13 years Boys 11-14 years	Middle Adolescence Girls 13-16 years Boys 14-17 years	Late Adolescence Girls 16-21 years Boys 17-21 years
• Rejection of childhood things, resentment when treated like a child • Preoccupation with physical changes and critical of appearance • Rule and limit testing – challenging parental authority • Argumentative • Moody • Risk taking behaviors may emerge (experimenting with tobacco, alcohol, not wearing a helmet) • Friendships are important – same gender friends and opposite gender group activities • Peers are used as a standard for "normal" appearance • Intense friendships of same gender • Exploring music, hair and clothes • Media and peer influences are high	• Often view themselves as invincible • Increased need for independence and "new experiences" • Process of gaining independence from family can be difficult, strong support within the family is critical • Self-centered: alternating between unrealistically high expectations and low self-esteem • Strong emphasis on belonging to the "right" peer group • Vulnerability to peer pressure • Looking to family, friends and other adults to help establish an identity • Extremely concerned with appearance, body shape and size, and sexual attractiveness	• Body image and gender role definition more secured • Self-regulation of self-esteem • Ability to delay gratification • Become more independent and emotionally stable • Choices and identity are less influenced by peers • Greater acceptance of social institutions and cultural traditions • Risk taking behaviors continue to emerge (drug use, distracted driving)

6

Sexual Development – Changing Desires

Sexual development is an expected and natural part of a teen growing into a young adult. Healthy sexual development is the combination of:

- Physical development of sexual characteristics — enlarged breasts for girls and enlarged penis and testicles for boys.

- Age appropriate sexual behaviors — kissing, touching.

- The formation of a positive sexual identity — who they are attracted to romantically and sexually.

- A sense of sexual well-being — a combination of: developed sexual characteristics, positive decisions about sexual behaviors, and sexual identity.

During adolescence, teens strive to become comfortable with their changing bodies and to make healthy and safe decisions about what sexual activities (if any) they want to engage in.

Talking with, not at, your teen about sex is very important — start in early adolescence. As parents, we wish we had total control over whether or not our teens are having sex. We know all of the consequences of sex before marriage or before being in an adult, committed relationship. But a teen's decision about engaging in sexual activity is not our decision. Unless we are connected to their hip 24/7, teens will find opportunities to engage in sexual activities if they choose.

As parents, if we are not talking with our teens about healthy sexuality, who will? Their information will come from their friends, the internet and the media.

Teen decisions about sex are dependent on:

- **Personal readiness:** Thought out decisions about what sexual activities they will participate (or not participate) in prior to having the opportunity. **The more teens think about what they are going to do in a given situation, the more likely they will follow through with this plan.**

- **Family standards:** Discussions of expectations related to sexual activities. Approach this using strategies that help to ensure your teen will hear what you are telling them. Start by saying something like, *"I know it is your decision. I care about you and hope that you will wait to have sex until (college, marriage, you are in a committed relationship)"*. Let them know your reasons for this, without going into a long story.

- **Past exposure to sexual abuse:** Teens who have been abused are more likely to engage in sexual activities.

- **Peer pressure:** Friends' and partner's feelings about sex.

- **Religious values:** Strong, internalized values of chastity will delay initiation of sexual activities.

- **Having the opportunity:** A willing partner and somewhere to go (most commonly this is an empty house between the hours when school ends and a parent gets home from work.)

What is influencing teens to engage in sexual activity? Biological and hormonal urges, curiosity, and a desire for social acceptance. There is also an added societal pressure for girls to be sexy in all parts of their lives and for guys to notice and act on this. Society is sending our teens very mixed messages about how they should look and act, many times contradicting what parents are telling them at home. This makes it difficult for teens to develop a healthy sexual identity.

Guiding teens toward making healthy decisions about sex can be difficult. It can be an emotionally charged discussion, especially if you feel strongly that your son or daughter should wait to have sex. The more you use the common tactic of telling your son or daughter not to have sex, the more likely that they will want to do it. The best approach is to start early and talk about it often!

■ ■ ■

Here are some suggestions on how to guide your teens toward healthy sexual decisions:

- Encourage your teen to love and value themselves. You may think they love themselves a little too much sometimes, but what they are showing everyone on the outside is often not what they are feeling inside. Teens struggle with their identity and all of the changes happening during puberty. This causes them to devalue or get down on themselves. When teens understand, accept and value themselves, they are less likely to engage in unsafe sex.

- Encourage your teen to leave nice at the door. Girls in particular are socialized to be nice at all costs and can ignore their needs, wants, and desires in favor of their partner's. It is important to teach your teen to be true to themselves and let their partner know what is right for them when it comes to sexual activities.

- Clearly express your expectations for their sexual behaviors and provide guidance, not directives.

  - Having an open discussion of reasons for and against having sex can help teens understand the advantages of delaying sexual activity until they are more mature and prepared.

  - Validate that there are benefits to having a healthy, loving sexual relationship (physical pleasure, emotional connection). It is important for you to include these or other benefits (briefly) at the beginning of your discussion, so that your son or daughter feels you are being authentic and acknowledging reasons why they might be considering engaging in sexual activities.

  - Then focus your discussion on the potential negatives — not just disease and pregnancy, but also emotional commitment, heartbreak, damage to reputations, loss of trust of parents, more stress. At the end of the discussion, share with them your expectations: "*I love you, and as your parent, I hope that you will wait to have sex until you are at least out of high school and in a committed relationship.*" A statement like this clearly describes your expectations with the acknowledgement that they have control over their behaviors. Although not as easy as telling them, "*Don't have sex or else...*" this approach is more likely to delay teen sexual behaviors.

Another key piece of sexual development is defining one's gender and sexual identity. Because identity develops across the lifespan, adolescence is a period in which teens may still be uncertain of their sexual or gender identity. This topic makes many parents uncomfortable, yet it is important for parents to know and understand sexual and gender identity and what the different words mean.

Sexual identity is a person's romantic and sexual attraction to others based on their gender — meaning who they are attracted to: boys, girls or both. Sexual identity is typically defined as heterosexual (straight), homosexual (gay), lesbian (gay woman), or bisexual (being attracted to both boys and girls). Sexual identity does **not** automatically equal sexual experience or behaviors. A teen can identify as gay and never have had a sexual experience with the same gender, just as a teen can identify as straight and never have had a sexual experience with the opposite gender. Sexual identity is an internal sense – it is *feelings of attraction* toward others, not sexual behaviors with others.

Gender identity describes a person's internal, deeply felt sense of being male, female, both, neither, or in between. This sense of gender (or gender identity) may or may not match the gender a person was born into. Transgender is a term used for a person that feels the gender they were born into is a false or incomplete description of their identity. For example, a person born as a man, that describes their gender identity as woman, would be considered a transgender woman.

Sorting out gender and sexual identity can be confusing, especially for teens. Lesbian, gay, bisexual, and transgender (or LGBT) teens are often bullied and stigmatized by people in their families, schools and communities. This mistreatment harms a teen's self-esteem and increases their risk for developing other more serious problems like depression leading to suicide and drug abuse. Because of these negative experiences LGBT teens may feel particularly alone, cut off, or even defective.

■ ■ ■

>> What you can do...

If your teen "comes out" to you as identifying as LGBT, the first step is to make sure they know that you love them no matter what their identity. You may respond initially with something like, "*I love you. Thank you for trusting me enough to share this with me.*" There are many resources to help parents understand and support their LGBT teen. See the *Parent and Teen Resources* section at the end of this book where you will find websites and hotline numbers for both LGBT teens and their parents.

■ ■ ■

Early Adolescence Girls 9-13 years Boys 11-14 years	Middle Adolescence Girls 13-16 years Boys 14-17 years	Late Adolescence Girls 16-21 years Boys 17-21 years
• Searching for new people to love in addition to parents • Sexual fantasies are common and may serve as a source of guilt • Masturbation begins during this period and may be accompanied by guilt • Worry about being "normal" • Gay, lesbian, bisexual and transgender (LGBT) youth may feel different without knowing why	• Experimentation with relationships and sexual behaviors • Frequently changing relationships with more emphasis on physical contact • Movement toward defining sexual identity, often accompanied by identity confusion and fears of homosexuality • LGBT teens may be bullied or feel left out, which can lead to problems such as depression, substance use and other risky behaviors • Sexual behaviors do not always match sexual identity or orientation	• Greater intimacy skills • More capable of intimate, complex relationships • Selection of partner based on their own preferences • Sexual identity becoming more secured • Sexual behavior becomes more expressive

7

Teens and Risky Behaviors – What Are They Doing?

Before I get into the details of how to talk with your teen about risky behaviors (coming in Section 2), it is important to understand a little more about risky behaviors and how they can affect your teen's health.

Most serious adult health issues are caused by disease, which is why adults are routinely screened for things like high blood pressure, cancer, and heart disease. **However for teens, the most serious health issues are not caused by disease, but instead result from their behaviors, experiences and feelings.** I am collectively calling these *risky behaviors* – something a teen is choosing to do, has experienced (has happened to them), or is feeling.

Every year statistics show that 75% (3 out of 4) teen and young adult deaths are due to their risky behaviors. Among the leading causes are:

- Motor vehicle crashes resulting from texting, alcohol or drug use.
- Homicide resulting from anger, abuse or bullying.
- Suicide resulting from depression or bullying.

In addition to this, 1 in 4 teens are at risk for substance abuse, sexually transmitted infections, early unintentional (accidental) pregnancy, and school failure. Despite these disheartening statistics, there is good news - unlike most disease, risky behaviors and their negative consequences are PREVENTABLE.

As previously discussed in the chapters on teen development, our sons and daughters are growing and changing dramatically during adolescence. Risky behaviors are beginning at earlier ages and as teens get older their behaviors get riskier. Tackling the issue of risky behaviors can be challenging.

As parents, we don't want to think about our son or daughter *at risk*. It's normal to feel overwhelmed by this thought – like we don't know what to do to get through to them – but you are already ahead of the game! You care about the health and well-being of your teen and are on your way to learning new ways of talking with them about difficult topics.

It may be obvious, but the first (and most important step) is to start the conversation. Easier said than done, right? Risky behaviors can be very sensitive and difficult for both teens and adults to talk about, especially as a parent invested in their well-being. It requires you to be knowledgeable about the kinds of risky behaviors teens typically engage in and to have ideas for ways to decrease or eliminate those risks.

At the same time you have to manage your emotions, particularly when you hear something that you really didn't want – or expect – to hear. Managing your emotions and reactions (facial expressions and body language) is critical to having a discussion that leads your teen towards choosing safer options rather than riskier behaviors.

Finally, you have to navigate all of these things *without* coming across as telling them what they *should* do!

Let's stop for a minute and take a deep breath.

You may be thinking, I'll never be able to do all of this in the heat of the moment! Don't worry, you will get lots of ideas in Section 2 of this book – and I recommend talking through several practice scenarios with your spouse, partner and friends (or even just in your own head) prior to the actual discussion with your teen. Practice is particularly helpful for topics you find difficult to discuss.

The key is to provide your son or daughter with **guidance** in their decision making – *and* encouragement to channel the positive aspects of their risk-taking energy into less dangerous and more constructive directions. Risk taking doesn't have to result in negative consequences to a teen's health or well-being. Consider the benefits of risk taking in a more positive situation – like encouraging a shy teen to join a club at school or an artistic teen to use their skills helping with a community project. Turning risk taking into a positive growth experience takes thought and concentrated efforts to find the right fit.

Helping your son or daughter make safer decisions when confronted with risky situations is easier when you have a strong relationship –

a difficult goal for parents to achieve during adolescence. If you haven't had the opportunity to solidify a relationship with your son or daughter, now is the time. If you have a solid relationship with your teen, continue to make it stronger.

Family closeness and attachment have been shown to be one of the most important factors in leading to less drug use, delayed sexual experiences, and fewer suicide attempts in teens. Keeping **family time** a priority and an expectation for teens is important. This can look like traditional family meals or it can be a family game night (board or video games), time in the car to and from school, check-ins at the end of the day before everyone gets too tired, watching a favorite movie, or any other activity that puts you in the same space as your teen on a routine basis.

≫ What you can do...

Use family time with your teen to provide opportunities for them to think through potential risky situations and practice their decision-making skills. **Studies show that if teens think through and plan for future risky situations they are more likely to make safer decisions.**

Here are some ways you can facilitate the planning process:

- Get your son or daughter actively practicing decision-making through role-playing – not acting out situations with you (there won't be many teens who would take that seriously), but having discussions during opportune moments during family time. Use a current event, an example might be a news story on an accident related to texting and driving. Instead of a typical parental response like, "*See! Look what happens when you text and drive,*" offer a response that empathizes with the situation:

- "*It can be really hard not to look at and respond to texts when you are driving.*" Then wait for your teen to respond (a few seconds of silence is normal – teens need time to process what you just said).

- Listen to their response without judgement. If they say something like, "*I can text fast, it doesn't affect my driving,*" or, "*Yeah, when I get a text, it is hard not to look,*" follow up with your concern: "*I worry about you when you are driving and don't want anything to happen to you. No text is worth your life.*"

- Let them respond, then ask questions to help them plan for future situations: "*What are some things you think you could do to keep from texting and driving?*"

- Offer some solutions of your own: "*What do you think about putting your phone in the glove box or putting it on 'Do Not Disturb' when you get in the car?*"

- End with, "*What could you commit to doing?*"

- Next time your son or daughter is getting ready to go out, remind them of the plan they committed to for not texting and driving. Keep your statement matter of fact like, "*Remember when we talked about texting and driving?*" Give them the opportunity to tell you their plan. Then, if they don't tell you, remind them of your discussion: "*You were going to keep your phone in the glove box whenever you are in the car driving.*"

Demonstrate to teens how to choose between competing pressures and demands by talking through the pros and cons of making a difficult decision. It can be helpful to write them down and give *weight* to each one.

■ ■ ■

An example might be a teen who is struggling academically and wants to join a team or club at school:

- Help them think of every possible pro and con of this decision and write them down on opposite sides of a piece of paper.

- Then ask your teen to cross out the items that are least important to their decision.

- When they have done that, have them circle the items that are most important. Don't give your opinion on what should, or should not be important.

- Discuss their circled items to help direct them in making a final decision.

Many teens live in the now. Show them the benefits of *future thinking* by anticipating difficult situations and planning in advance for how to handle them. You can find good opportunities for future thinking discussions at the dinner table or when you are in the car with your son or daughter.

There are many common scenarios you could discuss – being offered alcohol at a party, having to tell a friend "*no*" to something they want your teen to do, or feeling upset because of something someone said about them on social media.

■ ■ ■

An example of starting a discussion might sound like:

- "*A lot of teens are bullied on (insert most popular social media site). If you were feeling bad about something that was posted about you or someone else on (social media site), how would you handle that?*"

You may also include talking to them about creating *code words* or tell them to blame you with something like, "*My mom/dad won't let me,*" if they need to. These code words or blame can be used to help them get out of a situation. Code words are usually something your teen can say or text to you that alerts you to their needs without alerting their friends.

An example of this might be if your son or daughter was at a friend's house and the friend wanted to drink their parent's alcohol:

- Your teen could text you their predetermined code, "*What's up?*" (this phrase doesn't alert their friends to anything if it is seen) and you would know that it means to call them immediately.

- Instead of your teen saying, "*Can you pick me up? There is alcohol here and I want to leave,*" he or she might say to you, "*Why do I have to come home, I just got here,*" and you know to go and pick them up. You can find out more and discuss the reasons why once you have them safely home.

If you are concerned about your ability to remain impartial when discussing risky situations with your teen or that you will react to what your teen is sharing in a way that shuts down the conversation, you may want to reach out to a trusted professional — someone who is trained and has the ability and experience in talking with teens about risky behaviors. Your healthcare provider, or a nurse or health educator in their office, may be an option. You may have a teen center in your community or you could reach out to a school counselor.

When is Concern Warranted?

Often parents wonder when to seek out a professional for help in talking with their teens about risky behaviors and when they may need additional services like mental health counseling. It is not as easy as noticing signs that they are physically sick (like cold symptoms) and then taking them to a doctor or other healthcare provider.

Here are a few warning signs to look out for:

- Risky behaviors that begin at an early age (early adolescence).
- Risky behaviors that are ongoing and not what you would consider experimentation.
- Engagement in several or many risky behaviors – for example, drinking alcohol that leads to having unprotected or non-consensual sex.
- Relying on the behavior (such as alcohol or drug use) to help them deal with feelings of anxiety or depression or to forget about something that happened to them.
- Risky behaviors that happen with peers who normalize the behavior. This could be a friend group where everyone is smoking marijuana – "*Everyone's doing it,*" is what you hear and what they see when they are with this group.

While it is important for parents to talk about risk behaviors and scenarios directly with their teen, it is also important to make sure that your son or daughter has a physical examination every year, even if they are not playing sports. A physical exam that includes a risk behavior screening and is performed by a teen-friendly healthcare provider is an important part of maintaining your son's or daughter's health through their teen years.

Healthcare providers can be your biggest advocates in supporting the positive behavior messages you are giving at home. Before you make the appointment, ask the professional if they use a validated screening tool to do age-appropriate risk behavior assessment. Proper risk screening ensures they ASK the right questions of teens in a way that will help them feel most comfortable, so that they are honest in their responses. This allows healthcare providers to work in partnership with you and your teen to ensure they have the information and support needed to prevent serious injury, disease and premature death.

In the case of risky behaviors, the more trusted and trained adults in your teen's support network – the better!

■ ■ ■

Chapter 7 – Where to Start

✓ Risk taking doesn't have to have negative consequences to a teen's health or well-being. Look for opportunities to turn risk taking into a positive growth experience.

✓ Keep *family time* a priority and an expectation for teens! Family closeness and attachment have been shown to be one of the most important factors in leading to delayed sexual experiences, less drug use, and fewer suicide attempts in teens.

✓ If teens think through and plan for future risky situations, they are more likely to make safer decisions when those situations arise. Use family time with your teen to provide opportunities for them to think through risky situations and practice their decision-making skills.

✓ Work in partnership with a healthcare provider or other professional to support your teen in making safe, healthy decisions.

8

Changing Behaviors

For many parents, it feels most comfortable to start a discussion with your son or daughter about risky behaviors by stating the behavior (sex for example) and sharing all the reasons why your teen shouldn't be doing it. As counter-intuitive as it may seem, very few teens participate in a behavior without at least some knowledge of why it is unhealthy or what negative consequences may happen to them. You are probably not telling them anything they don't already know.

Knowledge (what teens know about the potential consequences of a behavior) has been shown to have **very little effect** on whether or not a teen decides to participate in risky behaviors. This actually makes sense if you think about some of the decisions we make as adults. For example, very few of us eat all of our recommended vegetables, or get the right amount of exercise every day – even though we *know* we should. So we cannot rely on knowledge or the potential negative consequences of a behavior alone to influence what teens will decide to do.

So what exactly *does* influence a teen's decision making around risky behaviors?

Despite everything I just shared – knowledge does play a small part in your son's or daughter's decision making – along with these factors:

- *Perception* of the risk of a behavior
- *Intention* to take part in a behavior or choose safer options
- And finally, their actual *actions*

These may seem like very psychological terms, and they are. There are professionals who devote their careers to understanding human behavior, why we engage in certain behaviors, and what we can do to change those behaviors. We have learned a lot from their work, and in this book in particular I am sharing what has been learned on how to make a positive impact when talking with teens about risky behaviors.

■ ■ ■

First, what do I mean by ***perception* of risk**? Essentially, this is how serious or concerned your son or daughter may feel about the consequences of a specific behavior – and their belief that those consequences will actually happen to them. A key factor influencing our perception is the immediacy (or closeness) of the possible consequences.

Consider some examples from our adult life. A person who has just been in a car accident related to texting is more likely to perceive the risks of texting and driving as high than a teen or young adult who texts and drives and has not been in such an accident. Someone who has had a pregnancy scare is more likely to use birth control every time they have sex after that scare, at least for a while. Another quirk of human behavior – the farther away we get from the event that increased our perception of risk, the less concerned we become.

Overall, these factors are key to remember when talking with teens – who, as we know, are living in the now. **Helping teens have a perception of the immediacy or closeness of consequences is especially important.** For teens, in order to avoid or change a behavior, the potential consequences often have to outweigh what they feel are the rewards or benefits. Consequences can be outside of your control, like getting in an accident or getting a ticket when texting and driving, and inside of your control, such as punishments, like losing driving privileges, imposed for a behavior.

■ ■ ■

Next, let's look at *intention*. This little word covers a whole lot of ground. Intention is influenced by a teen's motivation, planning, and general level of interest in making a change. Motivation is complex – any of us can be motivated for a number of reasons, both external (related to our environment, social network, etc.) and internal (things we want for ourselves).

Take work for example – we are often motivated to continue working for our paycheck (an external motivator) but, if we are lucky, we also get internal rewards such as personal challenge or satisfaction in our work. Teens making decisions around risk behaviors may be motivated by countless factors: to please their parents, impress their friends, to feel good or better, to feel less stressed, etc. **It is important to help teens by talking through their motivations** – *"What are some of your reasons for: waiting to have sex... using condoms every time you have sex...driving without texting"* – **and also their intentions to engage in positive (healthy) behaviors** – *"How likely is it that you will: wait to have sex...use condoms every time you have sex...drive without texting"*.

The last question about intention can be loaded. Many teens will tell you what you want to hear just so they don't have to talk with you about it or *"listen to a lecture"* as they would say. You might start with an empathetic statement first: *"It is hard for some teens to wait to have sex."* Then ask the questions shown above. "What are your reasons to wait?" and "How likely is it that you will wait to have sex until after high school?" This may help set the stage for a more open and honest discussion about your teen's motivations and intentions. Just remember, don't freak out if they tell you something you don't want to hear. Use some of the strategies in this book to help them think differently about unsafe decisions they are making.

When you have a teen who is motivated and intends to engage (or not engage) in a particular behavior, **planning is key** to ensuring they can follow through. Planning is often an easier area for parents to embrace because we do it all the time, as any parent can attest who has gotten a child out the door in the morning, on time and fully groomed, dressed, fed, and armed with homework and lunch!

The great news about planning is that research shows that a teen is more likely to follow through with a behavior (such as not having sex or using a condom every time they have sex) when they have thought through the steps they will need to take. The frustrating part for parents is that the teen has to do the thinking and planning themselves in order for it to stick. You do have a part to play though! You can help your son or daughter by discussing various scenarios – helping them work through possible solutions and brainstorm several alternative options – so they can think through the entire process and select a path that feels comfortable and achievable to them.

■ ■ ■

» **What you can do...**

This process can be used in planning for any type of behavior. We are going to walk through the following example:

Your son or daughter has made the decision to wait to have sex and is now in a romantic relationship...

- Start with an empathetic statement that includes a reminder of their planned behavior: "*It can be hard to wait to have sex when you are in a relationship and I know you are committed to doing that.*"

- Let them respond (remember you might need to allow a few seconds of silence for your teen to process what you just said).

- Then follow up with a question like, "*What do you feel you need in order to keep this commitment to yourself?*" This is the heart of planning ahead – thinking through the steps (what they need to do) in order to maintain or change a behavior.

- <u>Listen</u> to what they say (really listen – which can be hard to do when you are thinking of what to say next) – and offer suggestions they may not have thought about: "*Those are good ideas. Can I share some other things for you to think about?*" Asking permission gives them a sense of control over the discussion and a feeling of respect that you are talking *with* them and not at them. When permission is asked and given, teens are more open to hearing what you are telling them.

- Follow up by sharing ideas they may not have considered like:
  - Avoid being alone in a house with your romantic partner by inviting others to be there too; make sure a parent will be home; or suggest another place to hang out.
  - Talk with your partner about your decision to wait so that you are both on the same page.
  - Think through and practice ways to respond if your partner is pressuring you to have sex.

■ ■ ■

And finally, let's look at actual **actions.** What a teen has (or hasn't) done in the past can influence their decision making going forward. Previous actions or behaviors can influence a teen's belief that they can make a change and stick to it.

For example, if your daughter or son has performed well on standardized tests in the past, she or he will have a stronger belief that they will do well again. And the inverse also applies, as anyone who has struggled to lose weight or quit smoking can tell you. If you have failed at something in the past, you are less likely to believe you will be able to succeed at another attempt.

How much a teen believes in his or her ability to make, and sustain a change in their behavior is called their *self-efficacy.* The higher their self-efficacy the more likely they are to succeed in their planned decision. You can build their self-efficacy by helping your teen recognize wins – even small ones. You can also help them see how success in certain areas of their lives applies to other areas.

For example: *"It's great that you asked the teacher for more information about the assignment; asking for help isn't always easy but you did it!"* **Self-efficacy has been shown to be the biggest indicator of successful behavior change for teens.** The higher the self-efficacy, the more likely the teen will be able to change their behavior.

▪ ▪ ▪

Here's an example of how all of these constructs may work together, with the behavior of using condoms for a sexually active teen:

Knowledge: *"I know using a condom reduces my risk for getting a sexually transmitted infection, but really, how likely is it that I'll get something if I don't use one?"*

Perception: *"There were 334 teens living in my zip code that tested positive for a sexually transmitted infection last year. That's a lot."*

Intention: *"I'll get condoms from the clinic and keep them in my backpack so that I'll always have one available if I need it."*

Action: *"I used a condom the last time I had sex."*

▪ ▪ ▪

Tying it all together. I gave you a lot of information in this section, and as stated in the beginning of this chapter – information alone is not enough! I provided some tips and strategies to help you think through a plan that will work best for you and your son or daughter to have open discussions about risky behaviors. The key strategies to remember in helping your teen make and sustain a change in his or her risky behaviors are the *same principles that can guide you* in your behavior change to support them!

You can help support positive decision making in your teen, however in order to make and sustain a change in risk behavior a teen must:

- Have some basic understanding about the risky behavior and recognize it may be a problem for them.
- Believe that change will lead to an improvement.
- Have the internal motivation to make the change.
- Have the knowledge, resources and support to plan for change and follow through with it.
- Most importantly, have the self-efficacy (belief in themselves) that they can make the change happen!

■ ■ ■

Chapter 8 – Take Home Messages

✓ *Perception* of the risks of a behavior and *intention* to take part in a behavior or choose safer options, are the biggest influences on actual *actions* (behaviors) of our teens.

✓ When teens are guided to think through the steps to make a change or sustain a positive behavior, they are more likely to follow through with that plan (such as not having sex or using a condom every time they have sex).

✓ The more a teen believes in his or her ability to make and sustain a change in their behavior, the more likely they will be to succeed in their planned decision.

9

Strengths of Teens –
They Are Amazing!

Every teen has great gifts, talents, and resources, but human nature causes us to dwell on what we think is wrong with us instead of what is right – the same is true with parenting. We try to fix our kids rather than appreciating the abilities and strengths they have and expanding on those strengths to help them solve problems or change problem behaviors.

It is much more powerful (and longer lasting) for a teen to recognize a strength in themselves and use that to motivate their behaviors versus receive warnings you may give them.

- Strengths approach: *"Your school has a zero tolerance policy for parties and alcohol. You are really good at (insert sport) and want to be captain next year."*

- Versus warning: *"If you are caught at a party with alcohol, you won't be on the (insert sport) team next year."*

You are basically saying the same thing in the examples above – but the first bullet highlights (and ends with) their strengths and goals in order to give them an *internal* reason for choosing not to attend a party with alcohol. Part of our job as parents is to make sure our daughters and sons recognize their strengths and build on them. This will help to arm them with the self-esteem and self-worth needed to withstand pressures to engage in risky behaviors. It may feel overwhelming to try to focus on strengths, but don't worry, I will go into a lot more detail on how to do this in Section 2.

In its broadest and most basic sense, adopting a strengths-based approach to talking with your teenage daughter or son means modeling respect and kindness and conveying the belief that they have what it takes to continue their positive health behaviors (continuing to choose not to drink alcohol for example), or to make a behavior change when needed (such as committing to wear a seat belt every time they are riding in a car with friends).

Using a strengths-based approach will help improve communication with your daughter or son and help establish trust. Teens are more receptive to advice offered by someone who truly believes in their ability to succeed – an easy role for mom or dad!

Teens live up or down to our expectations.

Teens whose strengths are recognized will be motivated to develop those strengths. Teens who are always told something is wrong with them will wilt, and are more likely to use substances, report depression and anxiety, and have sex at an early age.

When we recognize the strengths our daughters and sons have, they are reassured that we don't view them as failures. Even though outwardly teens can be sarcastic and short (even disrespectful sometimes) when talking with us, they do value and internalize what we say to them. When we recognize our teen's strengths, we reinforce their ability to make healthy decisions. With a strengths-based approach, we are focusing on what is right and viewing our son or daughter in a positive light, which provides him or her with hope in times of stress or anxiety and gives them a foundation to build on when faced with decisions about risky behaviors.

Focusing on strengths takes effort – it doesn't come naturally or easily. Living with a teen is like being on a roller-coaster – there are lots of ups and downs. Sometimes we say things out of frustration – which happens – it is important to give ourselves a break, too. If we say things out of frustration often, try remembering to take a deep breath *before* responding in stressful situations. Our words have a **powerful impact** on our sons and daughters — both positive and negative.

A strengths-based approach starts with active listening. For example, if you want to engage your daughter or son in a conversation about a difficult topic, leading directly into the topic may cause them to shut down.

Instead of diving immediately into the issue, **begin by reflecting a strength** you know they have.

- *"You really care about your friend and want things to work out."*
- *"Some people give up when it gets hard, but you seem to be able to use tough times to grow stronger."*

It is important to make a statement that is authentic and could be backed up with *evidence*. Teens know when adults (especially parents) are not being authentic. My son would often respond to strengths I identified in him with, *"You have to say that, you're my mom."* So I would need to prove my statement with examples of when and how I recognized his strengths. My daughter, on the other hand, had no problem accepting strengths I was identifying in her and using them to grow stronger.

One technique is to use dinner or other family time as an opportunity to ask open ended questions to learn more about your teen and their strengths: *"Tell me something good about your day...something you are thankful for."*

"Nothing" may be a typical response to these types of questions. In that case, role model by responding for yourself – briefly share something you are thankful for, a good part of your day, or a strength you have that has helped you through a difficult situation. These kinds of questions and short examples are a great way to role model focusing on what is *right* rather than what is *wrong* each day. If they still aren't responding for themselves, give examples of what you see as their strengths or good parts of their day. Your persistence will be rewarded, eventually!

As discussed, the goals of a strengths-based approach are to raise your teen's awareness of their own developing strengths or skills, and then to use these strengths to help them improve their behaviors, health and well-being. You may be thinking: How am I going to elicit strengths? What if my teen isn't saying anything?

Try using a strategy from *The Circle of Courage*. This is an easy-to-use and effective framework to elicit, reflect, and build on the strengths of teens. *The Circle of Courage* covers strengths in these four essential areas (I have included some examples after each one):

- **Belonging** – feeling a part of supportive or trusting relationships: friends, family, clubs, teams, community groups, church.
- **Mastery** – recognizing skills or activities you enjoy or do well in: sports, academics, art, reading, music, cooking.
- **Independence** – having self-control and personal responsibility: self-care, current and future goals, exhibiting control when angry or upset.
- **Generosity** – giving of yourself or showing concern for others: giving back to others (neighbors, community, school), helping out at home.

Using this framework can help you identify some key areas of strengths and reflect those strengths back to your son or daughter. Teens need strengths in all areas to become healthy, productive adults.

Many teens don't recognize their strengths or have never heard them stated out loud (this is true for many adults as well). It can be an empowering experience. Strengths can help keep teens on track with making healthy decisions about risky behaviors, so it is important to balance both strengths and risks during your discussions with them.

■ ■ ■

≫ What you can do...

Here are some strategies for leading a discussion to help your teen learn to recognize and rely on their inner strengths when faced with risky situations – examples from each of the *Circle of Courage* areas are included in the suggested responses:

- Be mindful of opportunities to identify and reflect strengths during your daily interactions, not just when having discussions about risky behaviors

  - *"You studied hard this semester and it shows in your grades. You are on your way to getting into* (insert college goal)." (**Mastery**)

- Discuss strength areas that could use improvement

  - *"You really care about your friends. What does having a friend that supports you look like?"* (**Belonging**)

- Lead with strengths to help open or begin a discussion on risky behaviors

  - *"Music has been part of your life since middle school. Being named a drum major next year is an important goal for you."* (**Independence**)

- And point to strengths as a key part of any plan to change risky behaviors – both as motivation and support to sustain a change

  - *"You take care of your sister for us every day after school. She looks up to you and copies your behaviors."* (**Generosity**)

Then pause. Taking a moment gives teens the opportunity to think about what you said and process what that means in terms of their behaviors. Sometimes allowing moments of silence is the hardest thing for any of us to do. We feel compelled to fill the time with our thoughts, questions or advice, but developmentally teens need a little extra time to process their thoughts before they respond.

Once they have responded, share your concerns. Teens do appreciate it when adults are worried about them, as long as they don't think you are being controlling. For example, in the context of discussing alcohol use you might say, *"I'm worried. You're out with your friends a lot, going to houses you don't know well. Being caught somewhere with alcohol could get in the way of you going to (insert college goal)...being named drum major next year...your relationship...you being a role model for your sister."*

Allow them to respond, then ask permission to address the risk. This can be as simple as *"I would like to talk to you about drinking. Is that OK?... Can we do that now?...What time works best in your schedule today?"* It can be uncomfortable for a parent to ask their child for permission. There are different ways to do that based on the urgency of the situation or willingness of your teen to talk. As your son or daughter transitions to adulthood, this simple step gives them a sense of control and provides a bridge into meaningful discussions.

Finally, discuss the risk you are concerned about. I will introduce a model for communication called motivational interviewing in Section 2. Motivational interviewing can provide you with proven strategies for engaging (rather than shutting down) your teen – with the result being your daughter or son is making healthier decisions and thinking, *"Hmm...mom or dad actually 'gets me' and cares about what I think!"*

Chapter 9 – Where to Start

✓ In its broadest and most basic sense, adopting a strengths-based approach means modeling respect and kindness and conveying to your teen that he or she has what it takes to continue their positive health behaviors or to make a positive behavior change.

✓ Teens live up or down to our expectations. Focus on keeping a positive view of your son or daughter and share the strengths you see in them.

✓ It is much more powerful (and longer lasting) for a teen to recognize a strength in themselves and use that to motivate healthier behaviors.

Section 2

Talking With Your Teen

10

Proven Communication Strategies – Setting the Stage

Communication – a *shared* exchange of information – may feel more like a one-way street with teens. There are some proven approaches to communicating that can help you develop a meaningful **two-way conversation** with your son or daughter – it just takes practice and a LOT of patience - pretty much the recipe for parenting, right?

One of the most effective ways to communicate with teens is called motivational interviewing or MI. The strategies shared in this book are based on motivational interviewing theory. MI has been studied extensively by research professionals and shows promise as an effective approach with teens across a variety of risk behaviors including decreasing substance use, decreasing risky sexual behaviors, increasing healthy eating behaviors, increasing exercise, reducing stress, and reducing injuries and hospitalizations.

MI is different than traditional approaches to communication. It is not based on lecturing or telling a teen what to do and why, but instead focuses on getting teens to talk through and explore *their* reasons for and against a behavior.

Most teens know why they should or shouldn't be engaging in a particular behavior; in most cases when you lecture, you are not telling them anything they don't already know. Telling teens why they should or shouldn't do something causes them to tune you out – if you set the stage and **ask the right questions** instead of telling them why, **they will tell you** why they should make safer decisions about their behaviors and will argue for their own positive change. As an added benefit, **when *they tell you*, they are more likely to follow through and do it.**

No one does something "*just because*" or without a reason why, even though you may get a response like, "*I don't know*" when you ask your son or daughter why they have done something. "*I don't know*" is an automatic response to being asked "*why.*" It is a cop out to really digging in and thinking about your reasons for your behaviors. Don't allow your son or daughter to cop out by asking them why. Instead use different types of questions to get them to think more deeply about their reasons for and against engaging in a behavior. I explain this further in Chapter 12.

Let's try it ourselves, before we dig into how to use this approach with your teen. Think of a risky behavior you may engage in like unhealthy eating, driving over the speed limit, or not going to get regular health checkups. You already know all of the reasons why you should or should not engage in these behaviors; how helpful is it when someone tells you the reasons again?

Information alone is not enough to change a behavior and lecturing on all of the reasons for or against something is the least effective way to encourage change. Think about your risky behavior again and answer these questions: *What are your reasons for this behavior? What are some reasons you would want to make a positive change? What will it take in order for you to do it?*

Let's dig deeper into the example of eating healthy and practice asking ourselves these questions again:

- *What makes it difficult for you to eat healthy?* Some common reasons you may be thinking about might include: no time to shop, chauffeuring kids to practice and other commitments get in the way of cooking, it is much easier to pick up fast food when getting home late from work, unhealthy foods taste better (let's be honest)!

- We often get caught up with all of the reasons why we can't make a positive change and stop there, even though we know we should do it. Now think about your response to this question: *What are some reasons you want to eat healthier?* These are your motivations for making a change and can help keep you on track when it is getting difficult.

- Finally, *what are some small changes you could make to eat healthier?* Here's where it is important to know the difficulties (the reasons we examined in the first question), because overcoming these difficulties will be part of your planning for eating healthier.

■ ■ ■

>> What you can do...

Let's try this using an example of talking with your teen about wearing a seat belt when driving or riding in a car with their friends.

Traditional Approach: You doing most of the talking in the form of a lecture: *"You should always wear a seat belt...car accidents are the leading cause of death in teens. You and your friends are new drivers and are more likely to be in an accident. Even in the backseat you are not safe if you don't have a seat belt on. If you hit your head and hurt your brain there is no way to fix that – you will have a disability the rest of your life."*

MI Approach: Ask questions and reflect the teen's responses in order to **lead them into thinking about and <u>telling you</u>** why they need to wear a seatbelt. I'm sharing this example now before you learn about the individual MI strategies, to show you the difference in approaches (traditional versus MI). How to use these MI strategies will become clearer in the next few chapters.

- **Start** by asking, *"What is it about wearing a seat belt that you don't like?"* Knowing your teen's challenges to engaging in a safer behavior (like wearing a seatbelt) gives you a lens into their world and thinking process. Try not to respond immediately by giving them solutions to these challenges – just listen right now and remember what they share.

- **Next** ask, *"What are some reasons you would want to wear one?"* Listen to <u>their</u> reasons (motivations), many times they will be different from yours. You can reflect (or repeat back to them) these reasons (their motivations) to build on your son's or daughter's commitment to them. If they say they have no reasons, you may respond with something like, *"Getting hurt in a car accident would be OK with you."* This type of reflection is discussed in more detail in Chapter 17 and if used, must be done with a neutral tone of voice and as a statement, not a question. This type of response is meant to move your teen off of their *"I don't care or I don't know"* response.

- Then **follow up** with a key question: *"What would it take for you to wear a seatbelt every time you are in a car with your friends?"* Let them tell you what they need in order to make a change in their behavior. If they respond with, *"I don't know,"* or, *"Nothing,"* here is where you can reflect back to them the challenges they shared when they responded to your first question and follow it up with another key question: *"You don't want to be the only one in the car with a seatbelt on. What if you tried to get all of your friends to wear their seatbelts?"*

Using an MI approach like this helps to uncover their reasons or inner motivation(s) for making more positive (safer) decisions. MI helps tap into the mixed feelings and conflicting thoughts flooding most teens' brains to help them think through their reasons for and against engaging in a risky behavior.

As you know, teens act on impulse and rarely think through the pros and cons of their decisions. When you give your son or daughter the opportunity to think through their behaviors and voice out loud their motivations for choosing safer options, they are more likely to act on those safer decisions when faced with risky situations.

Using MI strategies is a great foundation for supporting your teen in making healthier decisions, but some teens are very resistant to changing an unsafe or unhealthy behavior. Your rules and punishments may come into play at this point – you might reflect their behavior choice and the consequences you will impose for that choice: *"Not wearing a seatbelt when you are with your friends is worth (insert your punishment)."* Remember to make this a statement with no sarcasm. Using this strategy, you are not threatening them with your punishment, instead you are stating it to them as a choice they are making.

By making this statement, you are causing them to think about the level of commitment they have to this behavior and then wrestle with whether the resulting consequence is worth their commitment. You will not hear,

"*You are right, it is not worth it,*" right away. End the discussion and give them time to think on their own. They may come back to you with some ideas for change once they have time to consider the consequences.

You may also have a time when your son's or daughter's behavior is very high risk and they need outside support. Getting help for your son or daughter may involve you working in partnership with a healthcare provider or trained counselor to provide maximum support for your teen, particularly if they are struggling with feelings of depression or anxiety, substance abuse, or eating disorders.

Teens consider health professionals the most reliable source of information and thus may be more open to seeking support from their healthcare provider. It is critical that your son or daughter feel safe in order to have an honest discussion about what they are experiencing or feeling. It can be difficult to achieve this as a parent because we have strong feelings about what they should or shouldn't be doing and it is hard to prevent those feelings from getting in the way, especially when we worry our teen may be in danger.

Recognizing when your son or daughter needs professional help is a huge step toward positive change.

■ ■ ■

Chapter 10 – Where to Start

✓ Information alone is not enough to change a behavior.

✓ Telling teens why they should or shouldn't do something causes them to tune you out. If you set the stage and ask the right questions instead, they will tell you why they should make safer decisions about their behaviors, and will be more likely to follow through with them.

✓ If your son or daughter is resistant to changing an unsafe or unhealthy behavior, your rules and punishments may come into play. Reflect their behavior choice and the consequences you will impose for that choice. This causes them to think more deeply about whether the resulting consequence is worth the behavior.

11

Building a Strong Foundation

Building a strong foundation for communicating with your teen is essential. A few months ago I was talking with a friend and she offered an analogy that nicely sums up our role as parents in fostering a relationship with our teens as they grow into adults:

As our children grow into teenagers and then young adults, our role changes from being their manager to being their adviser. When you create a solid foundation for communicating with them, you remain an expert adviser and someone they come to when they have difficulties long after you are done managing their lives.

The chapters included in this section will give you information and new ideas on how to build a strong foundation for communicating with your son or daughter. They will provide you with different communication strategies that you can use to have real (and sometimes difficult) conversations with your teen.

Before we dig into the details, I want you to know that if you feel overwhelmed by it all, welcome to the club. Learning new communication strategies brings up lots of thoughts and emotions like...I've been doing it wrong this whole time (which isn't the case, this is just a different way of *doing it*)...How can I ever remember all of this...How will my son or daughter respond...What if it works and they tell me things I'm not ready to hear?

All of these reactions are normal – even for healthcare professionals with years of experience. I would suggest that you not try to absorb everything the first time around and that you read through all of the chapters in this section to get an idea of the strategies – then go back and pick one strategy at a time (start with one that you feel most comfortable with) and start using it. *Where to Start* after each chapter will help guide you.

Don't limit your use to just your teens. The strategies in MI are a foundation for good communication with all of the people in your life – significant others, friends, coworkers — just about everyone.

Building a strong foundation for *Two Way Conversations*

Giving information is an important part of our work as parents. We have been teaching our kids about how the world works since they were born and it is difficult to pull back from doing that. The key is to remember your son or daughter is doing the hard work of becoming an adult and they want to figure things out for themselves. I'm sure you have already felt this push back from them.

Remember when they were 2 or 3 years old and wanted to put their own clothes or shoes on? You knew they weren't going to be able to button their shirt or tie their shoes, but they insisted on doing it anyway and got so angry with you if you didn't let them. Now that they are teenagers they are doing the same thing – only with other things that they want to be in control of like choosing what they do for fun or how they handle their stress.

The more you try to jump in and tell them what to do or how to do it, the less likely they will be to hear you. That doesn't mean you never teach or counsel them again. It means you approach the conversation in a way that your son or daughter will be more likely to hear you and talk with you. Again I am using the word *with* (talking *with* them) and not *to* them or *at* them to describe the conversation between you and your teen.

We know as parents that we have information through our own education or experiences that would help our teens think through a difficult decision or think differently about risky behaviors, but it is **only helpful if they are ready to hear it.** In this chapter I'm going to share some strategies with you to help build the foundation for your son or daughter to actually hear you when you are sharing information with them.

■ ■ ■

Building a strong foundation starts with *Asking Permission*

The key to sharing information with a teen is to begin by **asking permission**, especially if the teen hasn't initiated the conversation. Right now you are probably thinking, why would I ask my son or daughter for permission to tell them something? While this strategy may seem a little strange, try not to think about this as giving up your authority as a parent.

Remember that a normal part of development for your teen is their struggle for control. When teens (and even adults) are given the opportunity to say "*yes*" before you start talking (they are given control), they pay more attention to what you are saying. Just the act of saying it is OK for you to share the information makes them more open to actually hearing it, whether or not they really wanted to when they gave permission.

■ ■ ■

≫ What you can do...

For example, you might ask permission with phrases like:

- *"That same thing happened to me when I was a teen. Do you want to know what I did?"*
- *"Can I give you some ideas for (behavior change)?"*
- *"I would like to talk with you about...is that OK?"*

Don't be afraid of them saying "no." They may test you at first and say *"no"* to see what you will do. This is especially true if they are used to you talking *at* them by telling them what they need and not *with* them by giving them the opportunity to share their thoughts with you.

Most teens will respond positively to you asking permission by responding with *"yes,"* but if your daughter or son doesn't, it is important to respect their wishes and not force unwanted information upon them. If they do say *"no"* to your request, it doesn't have to stop the discussion. Follow up by asking what they already know about the situation or behavior. This can help get the conversation started even after their response of *"no"* to your request to share information.

■ ■ ■

Examples of ways to respond after your teen has said *"no"* when you asked permission to share information with them:

- You started by asking permission: *"There are lots of ways to handle this. Can I share some of the things I am thinking about?"*
- Your teen's response was, *"No, you don't understand."*
- Follow-up with, *"You are right, I wasn't there. Tell me what you think you should do."*

This approach respects their experiences and knowledge, and opens the door to more conversation. Approaching the discussion in this way, allows your teen to share their thoughts and ideas first. You can build on this (using strategies discussed later in this section) to keep the conversation going and eventually get to share the information you have. You might learn that they are already thinking about the things you wanted to share with them and now it is coming from them and not from you.

Once teens feel they have your respect (when you ask permission and allow them to talk first) they become more open to your ideas

and information. Even when they say they don't want to hear it in the beginning of your talk with them, most of the time you get to share your information eventually and at a point in the discussion when they are ready to hear and make a plan to act on it.

As you can see, asking permission can be a great way to start a discussion with your teen, but as parents, there are times when you need to talk with your teen and there really is no option for them to say "*no.*"

When "*no*" is not an option, you can still give your teen some control by asking them using a question like:

- "*I want to talk with you about (behavior or situation). When would be a good time for you today?*"

- "*You just got home from school and probably need some time to relax. I want to talk with you about (behavior or situation) after dinner, will that work for you?*" If they respond no, follow up by asking, "*We need to talk, so if after dinner doesn't work, when is a good time tonight?*"

What if you don't get a response? In the previous example on how to respond when your teen says "no" you followed up with, "*You are right, I wasn't there. Tell me what you think you should do.*" If you get a response like, "*I don't want to talk about it,*" you may need to go to a *when no is not an option* statement described above.

You may respond with something like, "*This is something we need to talk about. If now is not a good time, what would work better for you?*" If your teen responds with no time is good, try sharing your intentions for asking permission, "*I was trying to show you respect by giving you the opportunity to tell me what you think you should do, instead of me telling you, and some choice on when we talked about it.*"

Then pause. Let them respond to this statement – your genuineness may persuade them to give you a time they will be more open to having the discussion with you. That is the ultimate goal of asking permission – for your son or daughter to be more open to the information you are sharing. If they don't respond, you may need to continue with the discussion even without their permission depending on the urgency of the situation.

Try asking permission again in the future, particularly if there is a time when it would be OK for them to say no. Asking permission may be a new concept for your teen and will take time for them to come around and see you are making an effort to give them some control.

■ ■ ■

Building a strong foundation continues with how we *Give Information*.

When you are sharing information, make it brief and to the point. Remember with teens, it is all about them and they are not interested in your story even if it is a great one. Also, don't exaggerate the information for an effect – teens see right through that.

Provide **information that speaks to your son's or daughter's situation or behavior**, something they are actively doing or that is affecting them in the here and now — not in the future. This goes back to what was shared about adolescent cognitive development and concrete thinking in Chapter 4 – most teens are solidly in the here and now.

In order to share information that helps to increase a teen's knowledge about a particular behavior, or their perception of their risk related to that behavior, you may need to arm yourself with the facts. You can start with a quick search on the internet. Just be sure you are searching on legitimate websites such as government or national organization's websites. This will provide you with up to date information on a variety of topics and will increase both the credibility and the impact of the information – if your teen tries to refute it. I have shared some websites you could use to find more information about some of the most common risky behaviors in the *Parent and Teen Resources* section at the end of this book.

■ ■ ■

》 What you can do...

An example of providing factual, brief information might look like this:

- You are concerned about your son's or daughter's romantic relationship. You feel their partner is way too controlling and are worried that this relationship is not healthy for your teen.

- Your son or daughter denies that it is a problem and doesn't want to talk with you about it.

- You continue the conversation by asking them, *"What do you think a controlling boyfriend/girlfriend looks like?"* or *"What would make you think (partner's name) was being too controlling?"*

- A previous search of the internet (futureswithoutviolence.org) had uncovered the following information that you share with your teen, *"Did you know teens experience the highest rates of stalking and 1 in 3 teenage girls are victims of physical, emotional or verbal abuse from the person they are dating?"*

- Now make it more relevant for them: *"Think about yourself and five of your friends, 1 in 3 means that probably two of you have been or are in this kind of relationship."*

If you approached this discussion in the traditional way and told them you don't like the way their boyfriend/girlfriend is treating them, they would have gone into defense of their relationship instead. Sharing information by providing some brief facts and guiding your questions helps your son or daughter to think more deeply about the situation and what they want for themselves.

■ ■ ■

Building a strong foundation includes *Offering Concern.*

Based on everything I've shared so far, it may seem counterintuitive to voice your personal concerns about your son's or daughter's risk behaviors. **Teens feel safe and protected** when parents worry about them – as long as they don't feel you are trying to control them. It is tempting to try to persuade them with your concern, yet persuasion is likely to lead to resistance.

■ ■ ■

≫ What you can do...

Examples of positive expressions of concern might include:

- *"I've noticed* (partner's name) *calls and texts you all day and doesn't let you hang out with your friends without* (him/her) *there too. I'm really concerned about the way* (partner's name) *is treating you."*

- *"I'm really worried about you. You're stressed out and stretched to the limit by* (school, sports, work). *Being this stressed makes it hard for you to control your anger."*

When you offer concern, this creates an environment of understanding and support that invites your teen to share their thoughts, feelings, and emotions about their situation. When they are sharing after your offer of concern, you are listening for *change talk* (described in Chapter 15) and responding to change talk with strategies to get them to think more deeply about their behaviors and ways to positively change them.

Often teens feel we are "out to get them" with our rules and punishments. When we offer concern, we are sharing with them our motivations for responding to their behaviors. We are not looking for reasons to punish them, we love and want to protect them. Having this understanding of our motivation helps to lower their resistance to the information we want to share about their behaviors.

Another effective technique in offering concern is to **give your daughter or son permission to disagree with you.** This approach increases the chance that your teen will hear the information you want to share with them.

For example, you may want to use one of these sentence starters before you offer concern:

- *"This may or may not be something you are concerned about."*
- *"You may not agree with me on this."*

Try saying them out loud and then adding the examples of positive expressions of concern that were shared on the previous page.

No matter what strategies you use when offering concern, make sure you are comfortable and it feels genuine to you and your teen. The key is to make your offers of concern with a more neutral tone of voice – not sarcastic or overly dramatic. You want your teen to feel protected and cared for by your concern, not judged or smothered.

■ ■ ■

Building a strong foundation includes providing a *Menu of Options*

Sometimes our sons and daughters come to us to talk about a situation and are ready to share their ideas for changing a behavior or solving a problem. They are at a point where they **are more open to hearing what ideas you have** – they feel ready, willing and able to do whatever it takes to change.

At these times, you don't need to ask permission before giving them information, but remember to provide a variety (or menu) of options they can think about and decide what they would like to try.

Think about it like this: You are at a restaurant and deciding what to order – all of the options on the menu would solve your problem of hunger, but some sound better than others. The same idea is behind providing a *menu of options* for your teen to consider when looking to solve a problem or change a behavior.

Providing many options and asking your son or daughter what would work best for them is an especially effective approach for teens who are ready to make a change. It is hard not to jump in and provide a solution. Instead begin by asking your teen what they are thinking about doing and offer to brainstorm additional options or ideas.

Be sure to let your son or daughter identify and choose the one that sounds best to them. This can be the hardest part, because as parents we have opinions about what we think they should do based on our experiences and knowledge. Unfortunately, that is not always what they choose to do. **Remember, when they choose the option themselves, they are more likely to follow through and act on it.**

■ ■ ■

Chapter 11 – Where to Start

Begin by incorporating one of these strategies when talking with your teen. Then, when you are comfortable, add another.

- ✓ **Ask Permission** – Start with a phrase like, *"Can I share something with you?"* Just the act of your teen saying *"yes"* causes them to be more open to actually hearing the information you want to share.

- ✓ **Give Information Simply** – Provide brief, factual information that increases your teen's knowledge and perception of risk around a particular behavior.

- ✓ **Offer Concern** – *"I'm worried about you."* This creates an environment of support that invites your teen to share thoughts, feelings, and emotions about the situation.

- ✓ **Menu of Options** – *"There are a lot of things you could try (list out options). "Where do you think you should start?"* When teens choose the option they feel would work best for them, they are more likely to act on it.

12

Open-Ended Questions – Learning More From Your Teen

Communication strategies that work best are designed to encourage a teen's thoughts about a behavior and foster discussions around those behaviors. Basically, this is the idea that the more you talk about or commit to a behavior change, the more likely you are to try to do it.

An example in our own lives might be when we think about and then discuss dieting or exercise with our friends or family – discussing it *out loud* actually helps us move closer to engaging in eating healthier or exercise activities. If we were just to listen to our friends talk about dieting or exercise and not participate in the conversation, we are less likely to make a change. For many of us, giving *voice* to an idea adds an additional element of internal pressure to move forward.

In the following three chapters I will review a series of strategies that can help draw out thoughtful discussion and a commitment for positive change from your daughter or son. The easiest way to remember this series of strategies is by using an acronym **OAR**.

OAR stands for: **O**pen-ended questions, **A**ffirmations, and **R**eflections.

■ ■ ■

We will start by discussing **Open-ended questions**.

Open-ended questions are the backbone of learning more from your teen. They are questions that are not easily answered with a yes or no response. Open-ended questions set the tone for communication and allow teens to think through their risky behaviors and possible alternatives to those behaviors. Open-ended questions create forward momentum to help teens explore their reasons and options for change.

Many times the questions we ask teens are closed-ended – meaning they only require a yes or no response. Close-ended questions do nothing to move your conversation forward. In fact, teens report feeling *grilled* when asked closed-ended questions – which can lead to half truthful answers and can negatively affect your ability to develop the trusted relationship you are aiming for.

You've probably experienced this total shut-down from your daughter or son when asking about their school day with seemingly innocent questions like, "*Did you have a good day at school? Do you have homework? Was practice fun?*" Typical responses you get to these questions are "*yeah*" or "*it was fine.*"

■ ■ ■

Closed-ended questions can be directing and end up being a roadblock to communication. This type of questioning sets up the parent as the expert (and the one who is doing all of the work to keep the conversation going) and the teen is placed in the role of the passive recipient. Using open-ended questioning puts the teen in the role of expert of their own experiences and shifts the conversational work onto them as they think about and respond to questions.

The first step in changing how you ask questions from closed-ended to open-ended is to be aware and intentional when asking questions. Open-ended questions can be useful in gathering information and directing the conversation. A good open-ended question can lead to conversations about changing a risky behavior much more quickly than a closed-ended one.

For example asking, "*What would it take for you not to drink when you are somewhere that alcohol is being offered to you?*" will elicit your teen's own thoughts about risky situations versus a closed-ended question like, "*You are not going to drink alcohol if someone offers it to you right?*" Of course their automatic response to this closed-ended question is "*no,*" but even if that is their intention, they haven't thought through how they will be able to do it.

Teens are impulsive – if they haven't thought through the *how*, they are more likely to engage in risky behaviors.

Open-ended questions typically start with these words:

Who, What, When, Where, and How

Notice that the word "why" is absent. I'll explain this in a minute.

Examples of questions that lead teens to think about positive behavior change include:

- *Who can you count on to go with you to a party and not drink alcohol?*
- *What would it take for you to feel less stressed?*
- *When can you get your room cleaned?*
- *Where can you keep condoms so that you have them if you need them?*
- *How important is getting more exercise to you?*

An important part of helping your son or daughter make safer and healthier decisions is to find out their reasons and motivations for safer behaviors. That is where open-ended questions come in.

As a parent, one of the first questions we usually think of is *"Why?"* Even though *"Why"* questions are open-ended, they can have unintended overtones of criticism. Many of us remember being asked as a child when something had gone wrong, *"Why did you do that?"* You were being asked to explain something, which by implication, was your fault. *"Why?"* questions can be difficult to answer. When children, teens or adults are asked why they engage in a particular behavior, they frequently reply, *"I don't know."* The question assumes you had a clear reason – when in reality many teens have not actually thought through their reasons.

Instead, it can be helpful to start a *why* question like this: "**Help me understand** *why you have decided not to wear your helmet when you are riding your bike.*" That way the question is actually a statement, so it has less judgment. You can also try changing the *why* into a *what*: "**What** *made you decide not to wear a helmet when riding your bike?*"

Your tone of voice and body language are extremely important when you use a why statement. If your tone has even a hint of sarcasm, you just shut the door on any discussion around this topic. Your tone needs to be matter-of-fact, without any inflections or sarcasm. **Practice is very helpful here.** Try saying this example statement out loud in a matter-of-fact, sincere tone: *"Help me understand why you have decided not to wear your helmet when you are riding your bike."* Another set of ears in a friend or partner can help you practice your tone.

Sometimes, even when we are doing so well in using open-ended rather than closed-ended questions, teens will still respond with a one or two-word answer. Questions like, *"Where were you after school? Who was with you? What did you do?"* can make teens feel grilled and elicit responses such as, *"At the park...Jamie...nothing."*

Using a **fully open question can** instead help you learn more from your teen with less questioning by you. For example, you might use this statement: *"Tell me about going to the park after school."* That opens the door to getting more details about the situation (going to the park) and not just a one-word response.

■ ■ ■

Here are examples of fully open question starters (insert the behavior or situation after the starter):

- *What do you think about...*
- *Tell me about...*
- *How do you decide when to...*
- *How do you feel about...*
- *Help me understand...*

Be careful to not fall back on using one of these question starters repeatedly. For example, if you begin your question each time with the same statement, *"Tell me about..."* your son or daughter will quickly feel that the conversation is not authentic, and may even feel tricked when hearing the same phrase frequently. Remember to change it up!

Here are some examples of fully open questions that may help move your teen toward positive behavior change:

- *What do you think about using a helmet the next time you skate?*
- *Tell me about school.*
- *How do you decide when to post something on social media?*
- *How do you feel about getting more exercise?*
- *Help me understand your plan for getting control of your depression.*

Although fully open questions encourage more thought and discussion from your teen, it may take more effort to get some teens to talk. Another option you might consider are multiple-choice questions. This provides structure to the conversation, yet still offers teens a choice. An example may be, *"Are you upset by how you are being treated by your friends, fine with it, or maybe something else?"* Keep trying. Persistence will pay off as your teen comes to realize that you are interested and want them to share more about their behaviors and the motivations behind them.

▦ ▦ ▦

Finally, **key questions** are questions that move the focus of the conversation from the initial concept of building motivation to actually making a change, and ultimately to the stage of making a commitment to change. Key questions can test a teen's level of desire and commitment to positive behavior change. The essence of a key question is, *"What's next?"*

Examples of key questions include:

- *Given what you told me, what do you think you will do next?*
- *Where would you like to go from here?*
- *What will you do now?*
- *When do you see this changing for you?*
- *What if you tried...?*
- *What would it take to...?*
- *What do you plan on doing tonight?*

When you are using key questions, you may be tempted to push for action or argue for change. It is important to remember that the best action at this juncture is to simply listen, then respond with reflections (statements) of what your teen said in order to help solidify their commitment to change. We will explore reflections more in depth in Chapter 14.

▦ ▦ ▦

Chapter 12 – Where to Start

✓ Try using a fully open question like, "*Tell me about your day,*" next time your son or daughter comes home from school, instead of the typical question, "*How was your day?*" You should notice a big difference in what they share with you.

✓ Instead of asking "*why*" your son or daughter did or didn't do something...

- "*Why didn't you come home right after school?*"

✓ Try changing the "*why*" to "*what*" with a question like:

- "*What made you late coming home?*"

✓ Try a key question next time you want a commitment for safer behaviors from your son or daughter like, "*What would it take for you to wear your seat belt next time you are in the car with your friends?*"

13

Affirmations –
Focusing on the Positives

Affirmations are statements that recognize and show respect for your teen's strengths. It may feel like we've talked A LOT about the importance of recognizing and calling out your son's or daughter's strengths already in this book. But it's worth repeating – both as a reminder to ourselves, and out loud to your son or daughter.

Once you have identified your teen's strengths, you can use their strengths to encourage them, build your relationship, and help them see themselves in a more positive light — thereby building both self-esteem and self-worth.

Affirmations help remind teens of their personal characteristics, achievements, and experiences. These can be important attributes to help them make safer and healthier decisions. **I need to make an important clarification here that affirmations are not compliments**. To be effective, affirmations must be genuine and specific and be used to target a strength or support an effort.

Affirmations communicate an appreciation of your son or daughter for who they are. Affirming strengths reassures teens that you do not view them as failures and helps to give them the courage to change or avoid risky behaviors. For example, if your teen is struggling with a situation or trying to make a difficult behavior change you might use an affirmation like,

"*You are determined, despite setbacks, to* (insert change they are trying to make)."

Be careful — affirmations are like salt: a little makes things taste better; a lot makes them hard to swallow. Focus affirmations on the teen's strengths, effort, or intentions – never make them generic.

- A generic affirmation statement is something like, "*Great job getting an 'A' on your test!*"
- A statement that is more specific and targets your son's or daughter's strengths rephrases that affirming statement to something like, "*You are determined to get into* (insert college goal) *and studied hard to get an 'A' on your last test, great job!*"

The statement in the last example highlights the motivation and effort it took to achieve the A versus a generic "*great job!*" This helps to build your teen's belief in themselves and recognizes the strength and effort of their actions.

Affirmations don't use "*I*" statements – affirmations use "*you*" statements. For example, "*You have...you are...you feel...you believe.*" The use of "*you*" instead of "*I*" relocates the strength from an external (me telling you) to an internal focus (you have).

For example: "*I think you have the determination to make this happen,*" versus "*You have the determination to make this happen.*" Say both of these statements out loud and feel the difference in the meaning. In the first example, the focus is on what you as the parent think about your son or daughter, and in the second the focus is directly on the teen and their strengths.

■ ■ ■

》 What you can do...

Some examples of Affirmation Statements include:

You have...

...the experience to know that journaling about your day will help you process your feelings.

...the support you need from your friends to help you through this tough time.

You are...

...dedicated to being a good student.

...committed to exercising 3 days a week.

You feel...

> *...confident you can control your anger now.*

> *...it is important to be a good role model for your sister.*

You believe...

> *...wearing a seatbelt will keep you safer.*

> *...in helping others.*

Affirmations about a specific behavior, such as, "*You believe wearing a seatbelt will keep you safer,*" may be more acceptable when your teen is ready to change – what we call the preparation for change or action stage of behavior change. Affirming strengths and values may be more beneficial when teens are just thinking about change – what we call the contemplation stage.

Some affirmations for teens just thinking about change may include statements like, "*You value being in control of your body,*" or, "*You have support from your friends to help you pass this class.*"

You can also use previous successes to help affirm strengths and reorient a teen to what he or she has accomplished in the past. For example, "*Thinking about what you have been able to do in the past, you know what might work for you.*" Even repeated negative outcomes can be reframed to suggest persistence and a strong desire to change, with a statement like, "*Most people give up when things get hard; you are committed to seeing this through.*"

Even if a teen isn't ready to talk about changing – you can affirm that they are willing to talk about their behaviors. For example, you might say, "*Thank you for trusting me enough to talk about sex and condoms.*" That statement may go a long way toward building a relationship that will foster a continuing discussion around safer sex with your teen.

Lastly, be sure you are affirming the planning and individual steps necessary for achieving a change in behavior instead of just the outcome. Maybe you have an older or college-age teen or you know your teen is sexually active and you have had discussions about safer sex with them already. Instead of affirming your teen by saying, "*You are committed to keeping yourself safer by using condoms,*" be more detailed about what that takes by saying, "*You were able to get condoms, keep them with you, and have 'the talk' with your boyfriend/girlfriend about using them. You are committed to keeping yourself safe.*"

This is an example of affirming what it takes to achieve a positive behavior change instead of affirming the behavior itself. As a parent you should be talking with your teen about sex – whether that is focused on not having sex or being safer with sex is based on your beliefs and values and the relationship you foster with your son or daughter. Using affirmations to acknowledge their steps in achieving safer behaviors will help increase their belief that they can continue to do it and will help to establish a positive and supportive relationship between you and your son or daughter when having difficult conversations.

Chapter 13 – Where to Start

✓ Try using an affirmation to strengthen your teen's commitment to or their belief in something that they feel a part of:

• *"You have put a lot of effort into band this year and it shows."*

✓ When you are talking with your teen about committing to safer behaviors, use an affirming statement to remind them of their motivations such as, *"You care about your friends and want to keep them safe when they are in the car with you."*

14

Reflections –
Listening and Responding

Reflecting is the most valuable communication strategy you can learn — *and* one of the most difficult to master. Teens often perceive themselves as not being listened to, so when you use reflections as an essential part of your conversations, they feel you are finally listening to (and understanding) them.

The proper use of reflections can elicit more information sharing from your teen – even more so than open-ended questions.

At a basic level, reflecting involves **actively listening** to what your teen is sharing with you and **stating** back to them what you heard them say (reflections are not in question form), and adding to that reflective statement an emphasis, additional meaning, or continuation of their thought.

This *addition* to the reflective statement has two primary purposes:

- Expressing your interest, empathy, and understanding of your daughter's or son's needs.

- Creating momentum for and guiding your teen toward a positive behavior change.

Reflecting is an active, in-the-moment process. As you listen to your son or daughter, you will need to decide what to reflect back to them, what to ignore, and what to emphasize. Ideally if your daughter or son says anything about making a positive change in their behaviors you will want to reflect that back to them.

You can also use reflections to make a guess about what your teen means by a particular statement that they made. Making a guess is an important piece of reflecting. Remember that in Chapter 4, we learned that a normal part of cognitive development is that teens can have difficulties putting into words what they are thinking and how they are feeling. Reflections help teens think more deeply about what they are saying and feeling.

If you make a reflection and it isn't correct, your teen will correct you immediately. Being wrong in your reflection is not a bad thing. When teens correct your reflection, they share so much more. However, if your reflections are consistently wrong, that can feel frustrating to you both. You may need to practice with someone else a little more to get better at it before you go back to using reflections when talking with your teen.

There are several levels of reflection ranging from simple to more complex. The depth of reflection should match the situation. Different levels of reflections are used as teens demonstrate different levels of wanting to change – some types of reflections are more helpful when teens are resistant and others are more helpful when teens are talking about change.

To get started, let's focus on Simple Reflections – such as *Repeating, Rephrasing, Paraphrasing and Reflecting Feelings*.

A key component of reflections is that you allow **silence** following your reflective statement. This gives time for your teen to process what you just said and to respond. You will have to get comfortable with a few seconds of silence when using reflections and not filling that space with a question or personal story.

■ ■ ■

Examples of **Simple Reflections** shared below are based on the following scenario: **Your son or daughter struggles with depression and is having a particularly hard time right now.**

Repeat: The simplest form of reflection is to repeat back the actual words used by your daughter or son or to repeat an element of what they said.

The purpose of a repeat approach is to express to your son or daughter your understanding of what they said, to encourage further discussion, and a check to be sure you heard them correctly.

- *"You've been more depressed lately."* Silence...let them respond to this.

Rephrase: To apply the rephrase reflection, you will reflect back in your own words the meaning of what they have told you, staying close to what your teen has said.

The purpose of rephrasing is to reflect your understanding, encourage them to say more about the meaning, and to focus the conversation on some aspect of the meaning.

- *"Your sadness is getting worse and you don't know why."* Silence...let them respond to this.

Paraphrase: With the paraphrase reflection you are guessing at the meaning of what your teen has said. While we cannot mind-read, we know our teens and can make an educated guess at what is behind the problems they are sharing.

The purpose of paraphrasing is to verify your interpretation of what they shared, encourage more disclosure, or to focus on just one aspect of the problem.

- *"You would like to understand why you are feeling so sad."* Silence...let them respond to this.

Reflect Feelings: The technique of reflecting back emotion and feelings is the final kind of simple reflection. As a parent you may often suspect or feel sensitive to your daughter's or son's emotions.

The purpose of reflecting feelings is to *confirm* your interpretation of their feelings, to encourage more disclosure of feelings, or to focus on one particular feeling or emotion. For example:

- *"It's scary not to be able to control your feelings."* Silence...let them respond to this.

Think about each of these possible reflections and what you may learn from your teen. This is important because each reflection may take the discussion in a different direction. Use reflections thoughtfully to set the stage and direct the discussion with your teen instead of grilling them with questions.

■ ■ ■

Although you may be skeptical about whether this is a good strategy and be thinking it would be easier to just ask a question, reflections are more powerful than questions when discussing risky behaviors with teens. Teens will respond to your reflection statements. You don't have to frame them into questions.

- A good guide is to use 2-3 reflections for every question you ask.
- If your simple reflections are met with silence, resist the urge to fill the silence immediately with another reflection or question.

Remember, developmentally teens need time to process your statement and decide how to respond – it's actually an important skill for you to become comfortable with moments of silence! If they don't respond after a few seconds, it is OK to follow up with an open-ended question.

- With younger teens, reflecting feelings can be more useful due to their cognitive development.

How you use your tone of voice (inflection) at the end of your reflection is also extremely important. Whether your voice turns up at the end of a reflective sentence (which turns the statement into a question) or remains neutral or flat, can make or break the impact of your reflection.

Your goal is for your voice to remain neutral. Reflections can easily turn into questions without careful monitoring.

For example, imagine that your son or daughter tells you that one of their friends is having sex and not using condoms. You could respond with the same statement in one of two ways. You might say:

- *"Brad is not using condoms?"* Be careful not to freak out in your response. Your son or daughter is testing you to see your reaction.
- Or you could say, *"Brad is not using condoms."* Neutral reflection statement.

Many of us were taught to question in order to learn more – so your natural instinct may be to turn the reflection into a question to encourage a more detailed response. By turning your reflection into a question, teens may actually interpret that 1) you were not listening, 2) you were judging what they just told you, or 3) their behaviors or feelings are considered invalid or unreasonable.

■ ■ ■

» What you can do...

Because using reflections takes tons of practice, let's pretend you are reflecting information you just heard from your daughter or son. Remember, don't freak out in front of them.

I've included some reflections below based on behaviors that may cause parents to freak out. Practice saying these reflections out loud — first as a question, then try again in a neutral tone of voice as a <u>statement</u>:

- *You tried a sip of beer at Jackie's house.*
- *You are angry that you didn't make the basketball team.*
- *Wearing a helmet when you snowboard isn't something you want to do.*

Right now you may be thinking, what are any of these statements going to do to help my son or daughter move toward changing their behaviors? If so, I totally understand your confusion. Reflections may seem really out there or like something that is just not going to make a difference.

Let's walk through the first example – your teen shared with you that they tried alcohol at a friend's house.

- What if, rather than launching into a lecture on how they shouldn't have even tried the alcohol, how untrustworthy they are, and that they can never see Jackie again, you instead...
- Reflect back to them in a statement: "*You tried a sip of beer at Jackie's house,*" and then pause to let them continue.
- Your teen might respond with something like this:
  - "*Yeah, I didn't really want to, but her brother and his friends were drinking and they offered it to us. It tasted terrible! Jackie and I decided next time her brother was home with his friends we would hang out somewhere else.*"
- You can respond with another reflection or affirmation: "*You know you shouldn't have tried the beer. You have already planned what you will do next time so that you don't end up in that situation again.*"
- Then use open ended questions to talk about other ways to avoid drinking alcohol if or when they do find themselves in a similar situation. Now you are planning with your teen ways they can choose safer behaviors in the future.

You may not have gotten to a place where your teen is problem solving for the next time they are offered alcohol if you had begun with a lecture instead of with reflections. By initially responding to them with a reflection (instead of a lecture) you established trust. I'm not saying you will impose no consequences to their actions, just suggesting that you use another approach to discussing the situation initially before you talk about punishments.

Using this approach, you were able to learn more details of the situation. The next time your daughter or son is in trouble or in a situation where they need support, they will be more likely to talk with you. Most importantly, your teen will be more prepared to make safer decisions in the future.

Try thinking through the other three examples with the same lens as what I just shared. What might your son or daughter say after you make each statement and how will you use reflections to guide them toward safer behaviors?

■ ■ ■

Chapter 14 – Where to Start

✓ Allow a few seconds of silence after you make a reflective statement. This gives your son or daughter a chance to think about what you said and respond.

✓ Start with a simple reflection to show empathy (understanding): *"You had a hard day at school today."*

✓ Try a reflection based on what you hear from your son or daughter to lead them toward thinking about positive change: *"You are looking for other ways to manage your stress."*

15

Change Talk –
Let Them Tell You What
You Want to Hear

Change Talk is the collective words your teen says that support their interest or intention to make positive changes in their behaviors. The acronym *DARN* can provide an easy way to think about and identify change-talk.

When thinking about a change, teens first talk about what they want to do (*Desire*), how they would do it (*Ability*), why they are thinking about it (*Reasons*), and then how important it is to them (*Need*). As DARN statements are voiced out loud, commitment gradually strengthens, and teens may take initial steps toward change.

The same principles apply to our own lives – when we talk about a change we are planning to make with our friends or family, we make statements about our desire, ability, reasons and need and, by talking about it, we're more likely to follow through. By listening for DARN statements (change talk), you are learning more about your teen's deeply held values, and you are learning something about what they are hoping for in making the change.

A teen who says, "*I want to be a good student,*" or, "*I want to be someone my little sister can look up to,*" is telling you something about his or her desire. These are important themes worth exploring further. A deeply held value can be a powerful motivation and help them move forward in making a positive change.

■ ■ ■

» What you can do...

You can help to draw out DARN statements by using **open-ended questions.**

For example:

- *"How do you feel about wearing a helmet?"* (Desire)
- *"How would you start getting more exercise, if you decided to?"* (Ability)
- *"What would be your top two reasons for trying out for the team?"* (Reasons)
- *"How important is it for you to feel less depressed?"* (Need)

Be very careful asking about next steps and plans in this early phase of change talk. Notice I included, *"if you decided to,"* when I gave the example of exercising. You might also use a reflection before asking a question. For example, *"You are thinking about starting to exercise more, and you are not sure now is the right time. How would you start when you are ready?"*

Always reflect the change talk – even if it accompanies *sustain* talk. Sustain talk is talking about sticking with the behavior, or not making a change. For example, your daughter or son may say something like, *"I have condoms, but I am not sure I can talk to my partner about using them."*

This type of mixed message, or pre-commitment change talk (with the BUT) is very common. Don't let the BUT get in your way of focusing on the change talk. For example, you could use a reflective statement such as, *"You want to start using condoms. Your last step is to figure out a way to talk with your partner."*

You can reinforce the change talk, even if it's mixed in with sustain talk, by focusing on the action part of what your teen has said and not the part they view as hard. What you end your statement with is what your teen will continue talking about. You want to end with their motivation (their reasons why changing is important) or with the issue that needs to be resolved (in this example, how to talk with their partner).

Using an affirmation or positive statement about their skills or progress, along with an action-oriented reflection or open-ended question can be an effective strategy for encouraging change talk.

A statement you might hear from your teen is, *"I want to stop smoking, but my life is really stressful right now."* In this example you can incorporate an **affirmation and question** combination such as *"You are committed to stop smoking. How can I help you manage your stress?"*

Teens may also look to blame others for their behavior with comments like, *"I'm doing everything I can to pass math class. I would be able to focus more when I'm home if everyone would get off my back about it."*

It may be hard to identify the positive part of a statement like this, but it's important not to lose track of the change statement buried in the negative tone. You might say something like, "*You understand how important it is to pass math. You know what you need to do to make it happen.*" Making a reflection like this, stating back your interpretation of the meaning of what they said, prompts your teen to continue the story.

They may respond with, "*Yeah, I've been talking with the teacher, I have organized my binder with my notes, and I have started to put the test dates on my calendar.*" Now you have a discussion happening and you didn't get hung up arguing against their statement of *everyone getting off their back.*

■ ■ ■

>> **What you can do...**

Here are a series of strategies you can use to help bring about change talk from your teen:

Ask **evocative questions** – this involves asking an open-ended question in which the answer is likely to be change talk.

- "*What could you do to remember to wear your seatbelt?*"

■ ■ ■

Encourage elaboration – this is when you ask for more details when a change talk theme emerges.

- "*Help me understand how you are making sure you don't end up at a party where there is drinking?*"

■ ■ ■

Use an **importance ruler** – this is a simple technique to assess the importance of the change to your son or daughter, or their confidence in their ability to change.

- You might ask, "*On a scale of 1-10, with 10 being '100% absolutely yes' and 1 being 'no, not at all', how important is it for you to start exercising?*" OR "*How confident are you that you will follow your plan to do 50 push-ups and 50 sit ups every Monday, Wednesday, and Saturday?*"

- Then explore the number your teen gives you to elicit more change talk by choosing one or two numbers below the number they selected. For example, if the number given was 6 you might ask, *"What put you at a 6 and not a 4?"* This will encourage your daughter or son to describe their strengths or attributes and their reasons for change, which is more change talk.

- You can use the same approach to continue the conversation by choosing one or two numbers above the number your son or daughter selected. In this example, you might ask, *"What would it take to get you to an 8?"* This is designed to help them think through what they feel they need in order to make that behavior change.

■ ■ ■

You might also try an exploration of **decisional balance** – this technique has a very formal title that simply means exploring the pros and cons of both changing and sustaining the behavior.

- *"What are the good (and bad) things about breaking up with your boyfriend/girlfriend?"*

- And then ask, *"What are the good (and bad) things about continuing to be in a relationship with them?"*

■ ■ ■

Querying extremes is when you start with your teen's current feelings about their behavior and end with possible negative outcomes of the behavior. With this approach your son or daughter feels understood as to why they are engaging in a behavior **before** exploring the possible advantages to changing the behavior.

- *"What do you like about texting and driving?"*

- And then ask, *"What are some of the worst things that could happen?"*

■ ■ ■

Looking back – ask about a time before the behavior started. This is to be a reminder of how their life may have been better in the past and can get them thinking about making a positive change, in order to be able to go back.

- *"How much fun were you having with your friends before you got involved with your boyfriend/girlfriend and you couldn't hang out with them anymore?"*

It can also be used to highlight the positive effects after a change was made. The following example of looking back is a reminder of negative things that were happening and why they made a positive change, to help motivate teens to stay on track with that change.

- *"What was it like before you started taking your depression medication?"*

■ ■ ■

Looking forward – ask what may happen if things continue as they are and if they change.

- *"What if you stopped taking your medication, what would that look like for you?"*
- Then ask, *"When you are able to manage your depression, what does that look like? How is your life different?"*

■ ■ ■

Exploring goals and values – this is in two parts, first exploring your son's or daughter's goals and values, and then exploring how their current behavior fits within those goals and values.

Step 1 is exploring goals and values.

- Start by asking, *"What do you care about most?"* or, *"What is most important to you right now?"*
- Then reflect back their response: *"Being someone your little sister can look up to is really important to you."*

Step 2 is exploring how their behavior is affecting their stated goal or values.

- *"How do you think your sister feels when she sees you hungover from drinking the night before?"* Neutral tone of voice and body language are EXTREMELY important to being successful with this approach.

Using this technique of creating discrepancies between what a teen wants and how they are acting is highly correlated with behavior change – which is understandable if you think back about adolescent development and their new abilities to analyze what behaviors may or may not be in alignment with their own values and beliefs.

■ ■ ■

Chapter 15 – Where to Start

✓ Identifying or drawing out change talk (talk about positive change or behaviors) is key to your son or daughter making safer choices when faced with a risky situation.

✓ Look for an opportunity to have a discussion about a topic you are concerned about. That might be when your teen brings something up from their health class or shares a story about something that happened at school. Give a simple reflection of what they shared, then ask a question like, *"That sounds like a messy situation. What would your reasons be for waiting to have sex?"*

✓ Decisional balance is a good place to start when you would like to bring about change talk from your son or daughter. This strategy helps them think through the pros and cons of a decision or behavior and gives you a place to start the discussion.

Section 2

Final Thoughts

In Section 2, I have shared some MI communication strategies to help your son or daughter think more deeply about behaviors and their own motivations for wanting to change. Obviously some behaviors are more detrimental to your teen's health and well-being than others.

These strategies are not the only way to communicate with your teen about risky behaviors. You may have household rules and punishments that will follow use of some of these strategies if your son or daughter engages in your hot button behaviors. I'm not suggesting that you toss all of that aside – we are still parents. Choose your battles with the behaviors that you feel most strongly about (your high priority behaviors).

Teens will test their limits and make decisions that we wish they wouldn't. I have reminded my own daughter and son many times of behaviors I want them to avoid by saying things like, "*I'm not going to be at your side 24/7. You will be making your own decisions about whether or not to (drink at a party, have sex, text and drive). As your mom I love you and want you to be safe. What I hope is that you choose to (insert parent values) and if you don't (insert potential consequences).*"

This can be stated very matter of fact and without judgment or accusing tones. Of course, it is much easier to have this conversation when you have had years' worth of discussions around those *high priority* behaviors, but it is never too late to start!

Section 3

Avoiding Common Pitfalls

16

Planning for Success

It is difficult for teens to think through their options and make a plan for how they are going to change a behavior. All the talking in the world won't make much of a difference if your teen isn't developing a plan and commitment for safer (healthier) behaviors.

Teens struggle with thinking through situations and <u>planning ahead</u> for how they will handle difficult situations they encounter, like what they will do if they are offered marijuana, or if they find themselves in a home without an adult around and they are being pressured to have sex. These are very common situations for teens, and if they haven't thought through how they will respond, they are more likely to allow themselves to be pressured into doing something they didn't intend to do.

Studies show that if teens have the opportunity to talk through common risky situations and think about the different ways they could handle them, they are more likely to choose safer (healthier) behavior options when encountering those situations and are less likely to do something on impulse. We know how impulsive teens can be.

The key is planning ahead! Most important is that *they* are coming up with options for safer behaviors that are realistic for them – and we (as parents) are guiding them and providing additional options using strategies discussed within the chapters in Section 2.

There are many ways to change a behavior and think through possible safer options when finding yourself in a risky situation. Brainstorming ideas is helpful to allow your daughter or son the opportunity to make suggestions and think about what would work for them. As I've discussed in previous chapters, allowing your teen to identify and select the best path forward is the most effective strategy for them to make a safer decision and sustain a positive behavior change.

Instead of you suggesting one or two options for your teen to change a behavior or to use when encountering a risky situation, which often leads to your teen reacting to what is wrong with your suggestions, or listing all of the reasons why they can't do it that way, try asking some open-ended questions to kick-start the brainstorming process.

■ ■ ■

≫ What you can do...

Open-ended questions may include:

- *What do you think you could do?*
- *What have you heard that other teens have done?*
- *What if you were to (refuse to smoke marijuana or leave a house when no adults are around), what would that take?*
- *Can I share with you some other ideas?* Note that this example uses the very important permission-based approach discussed in Chapter 11.

These types of open-ended questions can be used to start the thinking process, particularly if you have a hypothetical situation that you are asking your son or daughter to practice how they might respond.

■ ■ ■

Try an example on yourself with this situation: You are planning a night out with friends next weekend and know you will be drinking alcohol. How will you get home safely? *This is your goal behavior.* There are many options you could choose:

- If you are in a bigger city or not too far from home you might call a cab or use a ride-share service.
- You might designate someone in the group as the driver (who won't drink alcohol that night).

- You might decide to meet somewhere that is walking distance from your home or a friend's home with a plan to spend the night there.

- What other options can you come up with?

If you didn't plan ahead, some of these options might not be available to you and if you waited until that night and it was time to get home before you thought about it, even fewer options would be available. Thinking and planning ahead provide us with the greatest opportunities to choose safer behaviors.

When brainstorming with your teen, it may help them process suggestions by creating a visual list. As your son or daughter is sharing his or her ideas for options in response to a risky situation or when they would like to change a behavior, let them know you are going to write down what they are saying so that you don't miss anything.

As discussed in Chapter 4 on cognitive development, many teens are concrete thinkers and having information they can see can be very helpful to them in processing what they are saying. They can use this information to make decisions about how they will respond in different situations. It's important as you are writing down their ideas that you include everything – even if it's not an idea that you would suggest (or even if you think it's a bad idea).

After the initial brainstorming, look at the list with your teen – and ask them what looks like something they could do right away. "*Out of all these possibilities, which one feels easiest to you...What do you think you could do right away?*" Your teen needs to choose their own goals and the steps needed to create a plan for safer behaviors. Their plan should answer the question, "*What do I do now?*"

The best plan to us as parents is not always the one that our sons or daughters will choose. Encourage questions and discuss feelings about the possible options, maybe weighing those options in a decisional balance (how much does one option mean to the teen versus another.)

This is critical to encouraging ownership of their behavior change and for teens to be successful.

For any big change, small steps are important to achieving goals. Teens should consider how much they want, can, and will take each step. Self-confidence in their ability to achieve a behavior change is very important and can make or break the success of their plan. It's not unusual to talk through a plan with your daughter or son, and feel that they are ready to make it happen, only to have them tell you their confidence is a "2" out of 10 (10 being absolutely sure they can do it). Rulers were discussed in Chapter 15 and can be used to help you understand what your teen's confidence level is. Using rulers also gives you the opportunity to explore reasons for their confidence rating.

■ ■ ■

≫ What you can do...

We've talked about little steps, but what exactly goes into a full plan for behavior change? A complete plan includes thinking through and addressing the following components:

- Create a goal describing their behavior change or their plan when confronted with a risky situation.
- Identify the reasons for making this change (or plan).
- Identify barriers that may get in the way of achieving the goal – and identify *solutions* for those barriers.
- Identify the people who will actively support the change process (or plan).
- Describe specific steps needed to achieve the change (or plan).
- Measure the goal, for example: I know my plan is working if...
- The last step – ask your teen, "*How confident are you that you can make this happen?*"

A written behavior change plan may look something like the image below:

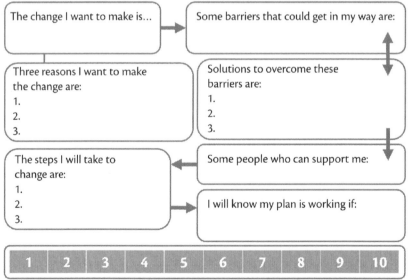

The change I want to make is...

Some barriers that could get in my way are:

Three reasons I want to make the change are:
1.
2.
3.

Solutions to overcome these barriers are:
1.
2.
3.

The steps I will take to change are:
1.
2.
3.

Some people who can support me:

I will know my plan is working if:

| 1 | 2 | 3 | 4 | 5 | 6 | 7 | 8 | 9 | 10 |

How confident are you that you can make this change?

■ ■ ■

Let's walk through creating a plan using a couple of scenarios.

An example change your son or daughter may like to make:

Your son or daughter is worried about their weight and wants to "*diet.*" When you hear this, instead of jumping in and telling them what they should or could do to eat healthy versus dieting (which would be a totally normal parental reaction), start by reflecting their statement with, "*You want to change how you look.*" Reflections were discussed in Chapter 14. This is an example of a paraphrase reflection. Hearing this reflection, your son or daughter will likely respond by telling you what they are hoping to achieve — weight loss for example, or a particular body change like a slimmer stomach or bigger muscles. They are telling you their motivation for dieting in response to your reflection statement.

Whether or not you agree with it or feel it is reasonable, try not to be judgmental. As parents we want our teens to eat healthy and be physically active. Focus on these behaviors as the ultimate outcome of their plan.

So, let's put this goal into our components for a behavior change plan:

- A statement of the change: I want to lose 5 pounds.
- The reasons for making this change: summer is coming, my pants are getting tight, I want to be healthier.
- Things that could get in the way: healthy food is not always available, it is hard to find time to exercise.
- Solutions to overcoming barriers: keep healthy snacks in my car (or backpack) like granola bars and apples; get more steps in by taking the long way to class and parking farther away; take a gym class in school.
- People who can support this change: mom and dad, friends (specific names are best).
- Steps to achieve the change:
    - Talk with mom and dad about buying healthy snacks.
    - Wear a fitness tracker or use a fitness app to monitor my activity and give me reminders.
    - Talk to my friends about taking gym as an elective.
- How will you know the plan is working: I lose 5 pounds by the summer.
- How confident are you that you can make this happen: 6

If you want to explore their confidence a little more to help them identify their strengths and support systems, you could ask, "*What put you at a 6 and not a 4?*" They will share with you the reasons why they believe they can do it (why they are a 6): "*I already put the fitness app on my phone, you said you would buy the snacks.*"

If you want to explore what else they might need to achieve this behavior change, you could ask, "*What would it take to get you to an 8?*" Your teen will share what they need: "*I need to plan ahead and put snacks in my backpack, and talk to my friends about taking gym and change my schedule for next semester.*"

■ ■ ■

An example of planning ahead for a risky situation:

Your son or daughter was texting a classmate who invited them over. When they got to their house, only the classmate was there – no parent or other adult was expected to be home for hours. The classmate starts to kiss your son or daughter and indicates they want to have sex.

- Planned behavior: I do not want to have casual sex.

- The reasons for this plan: I respect my body, I don't want a reputation as someone who has casual sex, I don't want to get a sexually transmitted infection.

- Things that could get in the way: it is hard to say no in the moment, there is no one else is in the house to help me if I need it.

- Solutions to overcoming barriers: practice ways to say no that I am comfortable with, ask who else is home before going to a classmate's house.

- People who can support this plan: mom and dad, my friends.

- Steps to achieve the plan:

  □ Use mom and dad as an excuse when faced with this situation: "Sorry, I can only stay a few minutes, I told my mom I would pick up milk she needs to finish dinner," or, "My dad would be really mad if he knew I was here, he might end up at the door if I stay too long... he's done that before."

  □ Ask questions about who will be there before meeting up at someone's house.

  □ Tell a friend where you are going and ask them to call you after you get there to check in on the situation.

  □ Have code words you can text when you need help. This was discussed in Chapter 7.

- How will you know the plan worked: I am able to avoid or get out of situations where I am being pressured to have sex and don't want to.

- How confident are you that you can make this happen: 8

These are two examples of common issues that teens struggle with, yet as you know there are so many more. Having a process for discussing behavior change and how to respond to risky situations is key to ensure your teen identifies what they want. It also gives them the opportunity to think through the steps needed to achieve their plan to keep themselves safe and healthy.

I'm sure in reading through the examples you had other ideas for barriers, solutions and steps to achieving these goals. If you talked with your son or daughter, they would have even more ideas.

■ ■ ■

Chapter 16 – Where to Start

✓ Let your teen take the lead when developing their behavior change plans so the plan is *theirs* and not yours.

✓ Start a discussion by asking something like, "*What would it take for you to* (insert risky situation to avoid)?

✓ When your teen does the work needed to develop a safer behavior plan, they are more likely to stick to that plan when encountering difficult situations!

17

Handling Difficult Behaviors – Introduction

All teens can be difficult in one way or another – and some teens push our buttons more often than not. This can make our interactions with them very tense and challenging. Dealing with difficult behaviors often causes parents to feel a variety of emotions – frustration, anger, anxiety, and despair to name a few.

Some common "difficult behaviors" of teens include:

- **Arguing** – this is the teen who is arguing against changing a behavior and in doing so, it feels as if he or she is challenging your accuracy, expertise or integrity. An example of an arguing teen, may sound something like, "*Marijuana is legal in a lot of states, what is the big deal if I tried it?*"

- **Interruptions** – this is the teen who breaks into what you are saying and interrupts in a defensive manner. An example of interruptions may sound something like this: you were in the middle of telling your son or daughter about a car accident you saw on the news and they break in with, "*I got it – don't text and drive!*"

- **Denying** – this is the teen that doesn't want to change, is not aggressive or defensive, but also is not recognizing that a problem exists. An example of denial may sound something like, "*Nobody wears a helmet when they are riding their bike. I don't need to do that – I'm not a baby!*"

- **Ignoring** – this is the teen that is yes-ing you to death, not paying attention, or giving one word responses. An example of ignoring may sound something like this: You just finished talking *to* (not *with* as I have been emphasizing throughout this book) your son or daughter about prom and all of the reasons why they need to be sure they are nowhere near and do not drink alcohol before, during or after prom. Their response is, "*I know.*"

As parents, we often feel like we don't know what to do or how to respond when our son or daughter is acting out one of these behaviors, or when we get one of these responses when trying to talk with them. The emotional response that parents have when dealing with these difficult behaviors is what causes us to shut down and avoid meaningful discussions *with* our teens. There are some strategies we can use that give us a chance to pause to gather our patience and respond to our teens in ways that will overcome common difficult behaviors and help us have more positive and meaningful discussions.

■ ■ ■

» What You Can Do...

Step 1 in overcoming difficult behaviors in our teens is to recognize the interpersonal tension – what exactly are they saying to you and how are they saying it?

- Are you hearing negative comments (as in the helmet example above)?
- Is your teen arguing with you to sustain their behavior (the marijuana example)?
- Are they sitting in silence (alcohol example)?

Recognizing this is important in how you proceed.

Step 2 is to monitor your own behavior and take a figurative step back. This is the hardest part! Pick your battles – if you truly want to have a meaningful conversation about a risky behavior, you have to be able to keep your cool. Way easier said than done, but so effective when you do it.

It is difficult for a teen to argue with you when you maintain a neutral stance. Arguing is like wrestling — it requires two people, both struggling to win, and if you stop, your teen can't continue to wrestle. It is like a forfeit or truce but it does not mean your teen has won.

Arguing and resistance occur in response to a perceived threat, and no one responds well to a threat. If you remain calm and neutral, your son or daughter will quickly calm down as well. In those times when they don't, you can reflect your own behavior and your desire to have a mutual discussion by saying something like, "*I'm respecting you by not talking to you in a sarcastic or angry tone, please respect me too.*" If you use this strategy – remember that you must say it in a neutral tone of voice and sincerely mean it.

Difficult teen behaviors can be reduced by you becoming less threatening in your communication, and acting to diffuse – rather than fuel your teen's resistance. This is difficult to do. As parents, our instincts are to react to these difficult behaviors. We often feel disrespected by our teens and want them to acknowledge their "*bad*" behaviors and agree with what we are telling them they should or should not be doing. There is a time and place for this type of parental oversight, but pick your battles.

It is better to act to diffuse your teen when discussing situations that you want them to think about and make a plan for change. Diffusing them helps to move them to a place where they are able to hear what you are saying and allows you to continue with a discussion on safer (healthier) behavior choices.

■ ■ ■

Here are a few questions you can use as a self-check when you find yourself arguing with your son or daughter:

- Am I dismissing my daughter's or son's feelings or concerns with statements like, "*Your life is not that stressful, that is no excuse for using marijuana*"?

From our perspective this is a factual statement, but developmentally teens are experiencing life as extremes. Something that feels like the end of the world to them is usually inconsequential to us.

Think to yourself – if I make this statement, where will it get us in our discussion on marijuana use? Ultimately you want to hear change talk from your teen that they will not use marijuana again. When you hear a statement like the "*Marijuana is legal, what the big deal? It helps me with my stress*" (or something similar) from your teen – focus on the underlying issues in the statement (stress in this example) and work to find other alternatives (to reduce stress).

- Am I acting like the expert and telling my daughter or son all of the consequences of their behaviors, with comments like, "*You need to stop, this is going to affect your grade point average and your ability to get into* (insert college),"?

Even though your statement is absolutely true – making your point with a statement like this will close the discussion between you and your teen before it even has the chance to begin.

Keep this self-check in mind when encountering difficult behaviors in your son or daughter: **the ultimate goal is to diffuse your teen in order to have a discussion that will lead them toward a positive behavior change.** When you can keep this at the front of your mind, it will be easier to let go of frustration and irritation with their behaviors and have a real talk with them about making safer or healthier choices.

Resistance from our son or daughter is hard to handle. We are parents, we know (for the most part) what is best for our teens and it is our job to tell them what to do or guide them in the right direction. What I am trying to share with the self-check above is not that you should stop guiding your teen, just do it in a way that causes less resistance from them so that they are more open to **hearing and then acting on** your guidance. The best way to manage resistance is to change your strategies.

There are a number of different strategies to break through the walls of resistance and guide your teen toward behavior change. I will discuss them in the following chapters. It may be easiest to try them out by role-playing with a trusted friend or partner before you try using them with your son or daughter. Some of these strategies may feel more comfortable to you than others.

You want to be as comfortable and sincere as possible when using these strategies, so it's OK to start with the strategies that are easiest for you.

Practice is helpful for gaining confidence with all of these strategies so you can use them whenever you need to. Some strategies may work better than others — with different teens and in different situations. You want to become as fluent as you can with as many strategies as possible.

In the next chapter, I am going to walk through specific strategies for managing difficult behaviors. These build on the strategies that were shared in Chapters 12-14: Open-ended questions, Affirmations, and Reflections (OAR). The more you practice these OAR strategies, the easier it will be to use them in more complex ways.

You can practice with anyone; remember motivational interviewing is a way to communicate that can be used with all of the people in your life – not just your teens. The more you use the strategies, the more they will become second nature and just part of the way you talk with everyone.

■ ■ ■

Chapter 17 – Where to Start

✓ Recognize difficult behaviors in your teen right away and monitor your reactions to them.

✓ Remain calm and act to diffuse their behaviors with a neutral voice and body language.

✓ When you can lower your teen's resistance to discussing a particular behavior or concern, they will be more open to hearing and then acting on your advice or guidance.

18

Handling Difficult Behaviors – Strategies

It is very frustrating to talk with your teen when they are exhibiting *difficult behaviors*. There are strategies you can use to help manage these behaviors and open the door to talking about positive behavior change.

■ ■ ■

» What You Can Do...

Let's start with something you have already heard (and maybe even been practicing) – **reflections**. There are several progressively sophisticated levels:

The first level of reflections is the *Simple Reflection*. You first heard about simple reflections in Chapter 14. The easiest way to respond to difficult behaviors is with a simple reflection. You don't have to stress or worry about what to say, you are basically repeating to your son or daughter what they just said to you.

Most teens expect adults to respond to them with directives or persuasion, so a reflection often stops them in their tracks. When you repeat back to them what you heard them say, it causes them to stop and consider it – teens often say things without thinking about their meaning.

Sometimes it is almost as if they don't know what they just said. Reflections help them to think more deeply about what they are saying.

As a nurse practitioner, I often counseled teens on their sexual health and behaviors. Many teens would tell me they were having sex and not using protection (not using condoms or birth control). At the same time, they would tell me that they didn't want to become a parent. I would reflect back to them something like, "*You are having sex and not using protection and you don't want to become a parent right now,*" – in a neutral tone and without judgement. Notice that I used the word "*and*" rather than the word "*but*" to connect the two reflection statements. Avoiding the word "*but*" is very important. Reflecting back these statements evenly and neutrally would cause them to stop and think. I could see the wheels turning in their heads as I observed them in a moment of silence. Then, the most common response I would get was, "*Yeah, it doesn't sound like that will work.*"

This reflection, repeating what I heard them say, opened the door to a discussion about abstinence, birth control options, and so forth. If I had jumped in with a lecture like, "*You are lucky you are not a parent already! You know that by having sex and not using protection you are putting yourself at risk for both sexually transmitted infections and pregnancy,*" that would have totally shut down the conversation with the result that the teen might have left my office in the same place as they arrived – engaging in risky sexual behaviors. If simple reflections are delivered with genuineness (again in a neutral tone and authentically), they often invite teens to elaborate without you having to ask a question or confront the behavior head on.

Even though your initial reaction or inclination may be to confront it head on, that will rarely lead your teen down a path of positive behavior change. They will dig in and resist you instead.

■ ■ ■

The next type of reflection is the *Omission Reflection*. This is most useful with teens when their resistance is represented non-verbally by a lack of communication (or ignoring behavior). The teen may be saying very little or responding with just a few terse words like, "*I know,*" and, "*It's fine.*" You can respond by pointing out the message their behavior is sending, for example with something like, "*You don't want to talk with me about what happened with Jamie on Facebook.*" Remember these are statements – there must be no inflection at the end making it a question. This is a very important part of reflecting.

Reflections are **not** as powerful if they sound like questions. When you make this same statement, but ask it as a question, you are making it easy for your teen to respond with, "*No.*" When you make it a statement, your teen will feel more compelled to *finish the story* and tell you why – in this example, why they don't want to talk with you about what happened on Facebook. A typical response from a teen to the reflection (not question) may be something like, "*Mr. Davison heard about it and already talked with us.*" As long as your son or daughter gives you more than a one word response, you can reflect their response and try again to start a discussion around it – "*Mr. Davison took care of everything and you feel good about how it was handled.*" This is an example of both a rephrase reflection and reflecting feelings. That will definitely get your teen talking – about either the details of why they agree with your reflection or why they don't.

■ ■ ■

The last reflection is an *Amplified Reflection*. These reflections can be tricky, because you MUST convey an attitude of empathy and not sarcasm. And the choice of words is critical – anything too extreme, or too overstated, or a reflection in the form of a question, may elicit further resistance. For example, listen to how important tone is in this example of an amplified reflection.

Say the following statement out loud: "*There is no reason for you to take your depression medication.*"

- Try it first with sarcasm.
- Next as a question.
- Finally as a neutral statement.

Notice how even though the statement never changed, the **feeling it conveyed** did change with each way you said it.

With amplified reflections, if your tone is straightforward and honest the MI approach will often elicit "*Yeah, but…*" statements, followed by reasons for change. In the previous example, "*There is no reason for you to take your depression medication,*" your teen may respond, "*Yeah, but I miss less school when I am taking them.*" Now you have a reason for positive behavior change and can reflect this potential reason, "*Getting through this school year is important to you.*"

You may be worried that your son or daughter will agree with your amplified reflection, "*There is no reason for you to take your depression medication,*" by saying something like, "*Yeah, I don't need to take the medication,*" rather than giving you a "*Yeah, but…*" response. Don't let this scare you away from using amplified reflections. If they agree there is still nothing lost. What the agreement tells you is more about the depth of your son's or daughter's attachment to their current behavior.

You may follow up by using another strategy to be sure your son or daughter doesn't think you agreed with them. You can say, *"I really worry about you when you don't take your medication. I know how hard it is for you and want you to feel better."* This is an example of offering concern – discussed in Chapter 11. You can also find out more about their level of commitment to the behavior (or status quo) and try to elicit change talk by asking, *"What would it take for you to make a commitment to take your medication every day?"*

■ ■ ■

>> What You Can Do...

The next strategy for managing resistance is another of the MI acronyms known as **DEARS**. DEARS stands for **D**eveloping Discrepancies, **E**mpathizing, **A**voiding Arguments, **R**olling with Resistance and finally, **S**upportive confrontation.

We'll start with **Developing Discrepancies.**

This strategy involves identifying, and even magnifying, the difference between the teen's stated values or goals and his or her current behaviors. Essentially this means shining a light on the differences between what they believe in and what they are doing. **Internal motivation for change occurs when teens perceive a mismatch between where they are and where they want to be.**

You can use these discrepancies to help teens become more aware of how their current behaviors may lead them away from their important goals. For example, if you know your son or daughter has been smoking cigarettes, you might say, *"You've been smoking cigarettes with your friends and at the same time smoking makes it harder to play basketball. Playing basketball in college is something you really want to do."* Again, remember to use the word "and" rather than the word "but" when you put the conflicting behavior with the goal it defeats.

Using "and" instead of "but" is very important. Then, try to let the statement sit for a few seconds. It takes teens some time to process the discrepancy you just stated. Be OK with the silence while they process. If you don't get a response, you could follow your statement up with another reflection like, *"Smoking could really get in the way of your dreams."*

When developing discrepancies, you can also use the phrase, *"On the* one hand (name the problem behavior) *and on the other hand* (identify their goal or dream it gets in the way of)." Think back to the example I gave in the simple reflections section about talking with my teen patients about unprotected sex. I also developed discrepancies using this strategy, "*On the one hand you are having sex and not using protection. On the other hand you don't want to be a parent right now.*" I know I sound like a broken record, but it is extremely important to frame these discrepancies as statements – not questions — and to deliver them with a completely non-judgmental attitude in both your word choice and in your non-verbal body language. After waiting a few seconds, if I didn't get a response to this reflection, or the response was, "*Yeah,*" I would follow up with a question like, "*Help me understand how this is going to work for you.*"

■ ■ ■

I would like to point out a few **key components when developing discrepancies:**

- It is important to always **end** with the statement that would **lead to change talk** (not sustain talk). The statement you end with is what your teen will continue to talk about. So, if you end the statement with, "*You smoke cigarettes to help you deal with stress,*" that is not going to lead your teen to talking about positive change. That will instead lead them to talk about how stressed they are and how much smoking cigarettes helps with that. When you end with, "*Smoking makes it harder to play basketball,*" it causes teens to jump on board with you – "*Yes, I really want to play basketball in college, maybe there are other ways I could deal with my stress instead of smoking.*"

- I want to re-emphasize the importance of using the word **AND** rather than *but* to connect the two statements. When you use the word *but* it can feel like you are disregarding the first part of the statement, whereas *and* respects the fact that they are both important to consider. Say each of these statements to yourself and think about how the conversation would continue following each statement:
  - "*You want to exercise, but homework is getting in the way.*"
  - "*You have a lot of homework and you want to make time to exercise.*"

When you use the word, "*and,*" be sure to conclude the statement with the positive behavior. Then you will be more likely to get your son or daughter talking about how to make the positive change happen.

Another way to develop discrepancies is by discussing the pros and cons of a behavior with questions like, "*What do you like about smoking cigarettes? What is harder for you when you smoke cigarettes?"* and end with something like, *"What else could you do besides smoking to feel less stressed?"* When you start by asking your daughter or son for their reasons for continuing a behavior, then move to reasons to stop, you establish a more trusting relationship.

Everyone has a reason (or reasons) for engaging in a risky behavior. Ignoring those reasons can cause teens to feel resistant and become unwilling to talk with you about positive behavior change. When you ask your teen about the pros AND cons of a behavior, you learn more about the barriers to changing that unhealthy behavior (like stopping smoking cigarettes). The barriers to change are their reasons for engaging in that behavior — what they like about it. Once you've listened to your teen's response, reflect what you heard, and then ask about the pros of changing that behavior, *"What are some good things that would happen if you quit smoking?"*

■ ■ ■

The next strategy in **DEARS** is to **Empathize**.

It is common for teens to experience a lack of acceptance and understanding from adults. Empathy is a fundamental and defining characteristic of MI. Empathy involves seeing the world through the eyes of teens, thinking about risky behaviors as a teen would, feeling things as they would, and sharing in the teen's experiences.

When teens talk with adults, our discussions with them typically focus on what they are doing wrong. This experience makes it especially important to convey a non-judgmental attitude when talking with teens. You adopt an attitude in which you attempt to see the world as the teen sees it. This increases their comfort in talking more openly with you about their behaviors and beliefs.

Empathy is expressed through skillful use of reflective listening (Chapter 14) and an attitude of acceptance of the teen's feelings and perspectives. **Acceptance is not agreement or approval**, but it does help to facilitate change.

Some examples of empathy include:

- *"It must be hard to stop cutting when all of your friends are doing it."*
- *"It is frustrating to have to take a pill every day."*
- *"I can't image dealing with all of the pressures of using social media."*

When you make an empathetic statement, you will be following it up with other OAR strategies (Chapters 12-14). You would not make an empathetic statement and then end the discussion. Using empathy creates a **safe and supportive environment** between you and your teen that you can use to build on to continue the discussion around a positive behavior change.

Let's take the last example of empathy:

"I can't image dealing with all of the pressures of using social media."

After pausing for your teen's response to this statement, you might continue with a reflection like, *"Using* (insert social media) *helps you feel connected to your friends and at the same time it makes you feel stressed."* Your reflection should be what you heard them say. This reflection would be an example of what you might have heard. Wait for their response, then follow up with, *"What else could you do to keep connected with your friends?"* or *"How could you change your use of* (insert most popular social media) *so that you feel less stressed?"*

■ ■ ■

Moving on with the strategies of **DEARS** we come to **Avoiding Arguments** and **Rolling with Resistance.**

Resistance occurs when there is a conflict between the teen's view of their behavior or the solution for positive behavior change and the adult's view — or when the teen feels their independence is being taken away. Teens (as well as adults) experience negative feelings when they perceive that they are being told what to do, or when they feel that they are being controlled.

Even when you want to make a change, if someone is telling you that you need to do it or how to do it (arguing with you for change), you start to feel like you might *not want* to do it! This is human nature unfortunately. Think about a change you have wanted to or have tried to make, one that you were considering but weren't 100% committed to yet. A common example of this is eating healthier or exercising more. Many adults decide at different points in their lives that they want to make exercise a priority (with different levels of commitment), and the more our significant other or good friends remind and try to encourage us to do it (with the best and nicest of intentions), the more it can irritate and frustrate us, causing us to give up and stop trying.

This is the same thing that happens with teens. Instead of pushing them to change, use reflections and open-ended questions to roll with resistance. This avoids arguments when resistance occurs and instead acts to de-escalate and avoid a negative interaction. **You stop arguing for change**

and instead encourage self-exploration of the behavior. This approach leaves little for the teen to resist.

For example if your son or daughter states he or she wants to go to a party with friends, you might respond, *"I'm not at your side 24/7 watching everything you do. We have talked a lot about different situations you might find yourself in."* This is a reflection that rolls with resistance and avoids arguments. Continue with open ended questions like, *"Tell me what you will do if you are offered a drink when you are at this party?"* to elicit planning for positive behaviors.

Additional strategies you can use to avoid arguments and roll with resistance include:

- Reframing statements to create new momentum. For example, if you hear something like this, *"Math is just too hard,"* you could respond with a reframe such as, *"You keep trying even when it's hard. Getting good grades is important to you."*

- Engaging your son or daughter in the problem solving. For example, *"You set a time to walk after dinner and your homework got in the way. Now you know that isn't going to work for you. What are some other ways to get exercise after school?"*

- Ensuring they understand your motivations. For example, if you hear something like this, *"Everyone else's parents are letting them go, you are ruining my life!"* rather than defending yourself, you could respond with an offering concern statement such as, *"I'm not trying to ruin your life, I'm saying no because I love you and want to keep you safe."*

- Changing your strategy in response to resistance. I've discussed many strategies within this section. Try them out to determine which works best with your daughter or son. Remember that as they get older, or their risk behaviors evolve, you may need to switch up your strategies accordingly.

■ ■ ■

The last strategy of DEARS is **Supportive confrontation**. This is a strategy similar to amplified reflections. It can be most effective when teens are withdrawing and not engaging with you (giving you the silent treatment) or arguing to sustain a behavior.

Consider a situation where supportive confrontation might be useful. For example, if your son or daughter shares the statement, *"Texting and driving is not a problem for anyone except old people,*" you might respond, "*You don't know anything that could happen to you if you text and drive.*" Be prepared, this approach using supportive confrontation can elicit a strong reaction from your teen like, "*I know all about texting and driving. I'm not going to get into an accident!*"

Keep your cool and use reflections that diffuse rather than fuel an argument. Try to reflect their possible motivation for behavior change and respond to their statement with something like, "*You want to keep yourself and your friends safe when they are in the car with you.*" This is an example of a paraphrase reflection from Chapter 14. This reflection makes a guess at their motivation and may open the door to elicit change talk and lead to a discussion of safer driving behaviors – where previously you were stuck.

■ ■ ■

›› What You Can Do...

Another technique for managing resistance is **Emphasizing Personal Control**. It is ultimately the responsibility of all teenagers to make their own behavior changes, and you as the parent have limited control over their decisions once they are out of your sight.

You can have a big role in helping them think through their behaviors, but to use motivational interviewing strategies successfully you first must be *heard* by your son or daughter. Use phrases like, "*You make your own decisions* (insert the behavior they are engaging in or choice they are making)....*I can't force you when I am not around....I'm not going to tell you what to do....You are in control of your body.*" These sentence starters emphasize personal control.

Once your teen feels you are giving them control, which they have to some degree whether you acknowledge it or not, they are more likely to listen to what you are saying and want to make safer or healthier decisions for themselves. It is human nature to want to take good care of yourself – it is acting on that instinct that we are trying to foster in our teens.

When you emphasize personal control, you can also give them permission to disagree with you, which further increases your chances of being heard. Use phrases like, "*This may not be a concern for you....You may not agree with me.*" Then continue your discussion of the behavior. This approach was discussed previously in Chapter 11.

■ ■ ■

Another strategy to put in your toolkit is the use of **Socratic Questions**.

Socrates was a 5th century philosopher who asked questions that led people to present their own arguments for change. The purpose of using these question starters as a strategy in working with teens to change unhealthy behaviors is to turn their energy of resistance into the first steps of positive change.

This sounds complicated but can be accomplished fairly easily by evoking critical, insightful thinking around aspects of their risky behaviors and incorporating this into your questioning. This approach is meant to raise awareness, promote reflection and improve problem solving around the risky behavior. You may bring in values and experiences that you feel would help move your son or daughter toward voicing change talk (Chapter 15) or you can choose to leave the question more general.

Examples of Socratic Questioning include:

- *What's the alternative...?*
- *What if ...?*
- *What would it take...?*
- *What's the evidence?*
- *What are the consequences?*

Ways of using Socratic questions when your teen is being resistant or when you are guiding them toward a behavior change can vary. Here are some examples using the question starters I just shared:

- ***What's the alternative...***

    ...to managing your stress if you stop smoking?

    ...to getting in shape if you are not able to find time to exercise?

- ***What if...***

    ...you continued to smoke marijuana for the rest of your life?

    ...you don't get your depression under control?

- ***What would it take?***
    ...Fighting feels like the only option right now. What would it take for you to feel safe without having to fight?

- ***What's the evidence?*** This one is a little tricky if your daughter or son is sharing with you their *street evidence* of why something is OK. For example, if they are arguing for using substances over long periods of time by telling you they know someone who did it without a problem, it can feel very disrespectful that they don't value your expertise related to this topic. However, it's important to avoid being caught up arguing with your knowledge of the facts. Instead try asking something like:

- ◦ *What would it take for you to believe that smoking marijuana causes health problems and can affect you getting or keeping a job?*

- With this approach, you are asking for the evidence **they** need instead of giving them the facts **you** know.

- ***What are the consequences?***

  - ◦ *What is the worst thing that could happen if you smoked marijuana for the rest of your life?*

  - ◦ *What is the worst thing that could happen if you ... don't get control of your anger... continue to text and drive... don't use condoms when you have sex?*

As you are listening to your teen's responses to your Socratic questions, use reflection statements to reflect back to them their values and experiences as well as any change talk you hear. This will help continue guiding them toward a positive behavior change.

■ ■ ■

≫ What You Can Do...

The last strategy is supporting your teen's **Self-efficacy**. Behavior change occurs when a teen feels that change is important and when he or she feels capable and confident in making the change.

Belief and confidence that change is possible (self-efficacy) is needed in order to make change happen. Parents can support self-efficacy by focusing on a teen's previous successes and by highlighting their skills and strengths in order to support their change efforts. You may want to review the strengths sections in this book (Chapters 9 and 13) for more details on how to elicit and reflect teen strengths.

- You can help support self-efficacy by reinforcing responsibility and your teen's ability to succeed going forward. For example, you might say, "*You have been successful at managing school and work in the past,*" or, "*I am interested in what you need in order to pass your math class.*"

- You can also cultivate self-efficacy by recognizing past successes and how they have helped your teen achieve their goals. For example, you might say, "*You are remembering to take your meds every day and are now starting to see a positive change in your school work and grades,"* or *"You feel in control of yourself now that you have limited your portions when eating meals and snacks."*

■ ■ ■

Chapter 18 – Where to Start

Begin by incorporating one of these strategies when talking with your teen. Then, when you are comfortable, add another.

✓ Developing discrepancies can be a powerful strategy. Start your reflection by stating their current behavior. Then connect it to their motivation for positive change using the word, *"and."* For example, *"You're having a hard time controlling your anger during practice and you want to be named captain of the football team this year."*

✓ Try an empathetic statement to show your teen that you understand their situation. *"It's hard to say no when your friends are saying yes."* Listen to their response, then continue with a reflection to lead them toward positive change talk.

✓ Use a Socratic question to elicit change talk like, *"What would it take for you to feel less stressed?"*

19

Handling Difficult Behaviors – Using the Strategies

Now that I have shared some of the strategies you can use for handling difficult behaviors, let's discuss strategies that may work better in particular situations or for specific behaviors. Remember every teen is different, so this is meant to be a guide that you can use to find the best approach that works for you and your daughter or son.

Let's revisit the common difficult behaviors previously discussed in Chapter 17:

Arguing – this is the teen who is arguing against changing a behavior and in doing so, it feels as if he or she is contesting your accuracy, expertise or integrity. *"Marijuana is legal in a lot of states, what is the big deal if I tried it?"*

It is normal to feel defensive, and to want to respond with, "**Because I told you not to!**" Pause instead because, if you respond in this way, you won't get any other discussion from your teen. Telling them not to do it didn't stop them from doing it the first time, right? There may be punishments you have decided on for this behavior, but before you go there, try instead to respond with **simple or amplified reflections or use Socratic questions**. These strategies can help get them to talk more about what happened and possibly move toward talk about not smoking next time they have the opportunity.

Here are some examples of using these strategies in response to your teen's arguing statement. Each strategy may take you in a different direction in the discussion you have with your teen. **Think about the direction you would want the discussion to go when reading through these examples.**

"Marijuana is legal in a lot of states, what is the big deal if I tried it?"

- **Simple Reflection**: *"You tried marijuana."* Not a question, a statement. This reflection is meant to elicit from your teen more information on the situation in which marijuana was tried, *"Yeah, I was at Sarah's house and her brother had some."*

- **Amplified Reflection**: *"Smoking marijuana would never be a problem for you."* Not a question, a statement. This reflection is meant to elicit from your teen what they know about the negative effects of marijuana that may lead them toward not smoking next time. Most, if not all, teens know at least some of the negative effects of smoking marijuana.

Making this statement will help to move them off of their stance on marijuana being *"no big deal."* Using an amplified reflection such as this, teens will typically respond by telling you what they know about the harmful side effects. You can then reflect what they say to keep them thinking through why they might not want to engage in this behavior. If they agree with your amplified reflection, you may want to offer concern (discussed in Chapter 11).

- **Socratic Question**: *"What would it take for you to not smoke marijuana the next time you get the chance?"* Using a Socratic question is meant to help teens think through positive behavior change and what it would take for them to commit to that change. **Listen for change talk** (DARN statements discussed in Chapter 15) when they respond to a Socratic question:

  - If they share **ability** like, *"I don't have to smoke, no one is forcing me,"* then you can reflect the ability you are hearing in their statement to make it even stronger with something like, *"You make your own decisions and you can pass if someone offers it to you."* As they agree with you, they may talk more about how they could refuse.

  - If they share **reasons** such as, *"I know I will be in trouble and will have to (insert punishment) if I do it again,"* then you can reflect their reason with something like, *"Smoking weed is not worth (your punishment)."* As they agree with your reflection, their commitment to their reason is becoming stronger.

  - If they share **needs** like, *"I don't want to get kicked off of the (insert sport) team,"* then you can reflect their need to help them think more deeply about it with, *"Playing (sport) is important to you. You don't want to let yourself or your team down by getting caught smoking marijuana."* Now you are giving them even more to think about related to need.

Interruptions – this is the teen who breaks into your dialogue and interrupts in a defensive manner. In our previous example, you were in the middle of telling your son or daughter about a car accident you saw on the news and they break in with, *"I got it – don't text and drive!"* By not responding defensively, you will gain their attention.

Use some of the **DEARS strategies** and **emphasize personal control** to help guide them in another direction. Here are some examples of using these different strategies in response to your teen's statement. Again, each one may take you in a different direction in the discussion you have with them.

"I got it – don't text and drive!"

- **Develop discrepancies:** *"It is important for you to keep in touch with your friends and you want to be a safe driver."* Let your son or daughter think about this and grapple with how that could work. **Listen for change talk** in their response.

- **Empathize:** *"It is hard to feel disconnected to everyone when you are driving."* Let them share their thoughts around what you just said. They may respond with something like, *"Yeah, depending on how long I'm in the car, people could think I'm mad at them because I'm not responding."*

Now you know a reason behind their texting and you can start to work on overcoming this. You might respond, *"It is easy to have misunderstandings with texting* (this is an example of empathizing with a rephrase reflection). *What do you think you could do to let them know you might not be responding when you are driving?"* Now you are asking them to give you actions they could take to overcome their reason for texting, and your son or daughter is on their way to safer behaviors.

- **Avoid arguments/Roll with resistance:** *"You don't want to talk about this right now."* Allow them to respond to your statement and change up your strategies based on what you just hear from them. Avoiding arguments and rolling with resistance is really about not getting into a wrestling match or tug of war with your son or daughter. As soon as you notice this is happening, take a step back with a long breath and change up your strategies.

- **Supportive Confrontation**: *"You don't know anything that could happen if you text and drive."* You were just sharing a news story about the consequences of texting and driving, so this will cause an immediate (probably aggressive) response from your teen. I have already used this example, but I will repeat it here. Your teen may say, "*I know all about texting and driving, I'm not going to get in an accident!*"

Keep your cool and use reflections that diffuse and try to get to a motivation for behavior change, such as, "*You want to keep yourself and your friends safe when they are in the car with you.*" This reflection may open the door to elicit **change talk** and lead to a discussion of safer driving behaviors – where previously you were stuck.

- **Emphasize personal control**: "*I'm not going to be with you every time you are in the car driving. You are in control of whether or not you text.*" By making this statement you are giving control over the behavior to your teen (which they already have) and that sense of control will cause them to think differently about the behavior. Now they feel more responsible for what happens if they choose to text and drive. Let your teen respond to your statement and **listen for change talk** that you can then reflect back to them.

Denying – this is the teen that doesn't want to change, is not aggressive or defensive, but also is not recognizing that a problem exists. "*Nobody wears a helmet when they are riding their bike. I don't need to do that – I'm not a baby!*" First and foremost – if you find yourself giving advice to your resistant daughter or son, stop immediately. Instead start the conversation by using **simple reflection, emphasizing personal control** and providing **supportive confrontation**. Here are some examples of using these different strategies in response to your teen's statement – each one may take you in a different direction in the discussion you have with them.

"Nobody wears a helmet when they are riding their bike. I don't need to do that – I'm not a baby!"

- **Simple Reflection:** "*You feel like you are too old to wear a helmet when you ride a bike.*" By using this reflection you are validating to your teen that you heard what they said, you are causing them to think more about their reason for not wearing a helmet, and you will probably elicit a response that tells you more about why your teen feels they are too old. They may respond with, "*Yeah, my friends make fun of me when I have a helmet on.*"

You can use another strategy at this point in the conversation, like an amplified reflection: "*It is more important what your friends think than for you to be safe.*" Remember a neutral statement is key in amplified reflections. Your teen will grapple with this statement. Then, when they respond, listen for change talk. These are times when they make the *"yeah, but"* statements (discussed in Chapter 15).

- **Emphasize personal control:** *"You want to decide whether or not to wear a helmet."* By making this statement, you are acknowledging their desire for control. Their response may lead you toward steps for behavior change, like starting with a few scenarios in which they can commit to wearing their helmet.

- **Supportive Confrontation:** *"There is never a time when you would need to wear a helmet when you ride a bike."* If they don't move off of this statement and you get a response like, *"No there isn't, I'm a good rider."* Then you can follow up with a Socratic question like, *"Helmets are not just about being safe. What if you picked one out that was cool looking and matched your bike?"* This is an example of how to handle instances when your teen agrees with your confrontation statement (or amplified reflection).

Ignoring – this is the teen that is *"yes-ing"* you to death, not paying attention, or giving one word responses. You just finished talking *to* (not *with*) your son or daughter about prom and all of the reasons why they need to be sure they are nowhere near and do not drink alcohol before, during or after prom. Their response is, *"I know"*.

Try using **omission reflections** and **supportive confrontation** to engage them in a discussion on behavior change. Here are some examples of using these different strategies in response to your teen's statement after you were talking with them about drinking alcohol on prom night – each one may take you in a different direction in the discussion you have with them.

"I know."

- **Omission Reflections:** *"You don't want to talk with me about this,"* stated matter of fact. The purpose of using an omission reflection is to prompt your son or daughter to finish the story by explaining the *why*, **without** you having to say, *"Why don't you want to talk with me?"* Their possible responses (reasons they don't want to talk) might be, *"You know I don't drink, it's annoying when you lecture me all of the time...The principal has already been making announcements about how anyone drinking at prom will not be able to walk at graduation, it is not worth it to me..."* Reflect this reason to make it even stronger for your teen: *"Walking at graduation is important to you."*

- **Supportive Confrontation:** *"You won't ever be in a position of having to say no to someone offering you alcohol."* Again, supportive confrontation can be useful to initially get your son or daughter talking with you (when they weren't previously). Use additional strategies when they respond to your statement to keep the discussion flowing. Do not use more than one supportive confrontation or amplified statement in the same conversation. That can be viewed as argumentative by your teen and send your discussion down a negative path.

Change is hard and helping your son or daughter make or plan for positive behaviors is even harder. The calmness at the heart of guiding is not always easy to achieve. The stronger your feelings of wanting your teen to change their behavior, the more mindful you need to be about your own behaviors. **You most likely will not be there to rescue them if they need it – you are equipping them with the ability to rescue themselves.**

Even with all of the tools and strategies you have read about in this book on how to have real talks with your teen about risky behaviors, there will still be times when the discussion is not going well and you need to take a break and walk away. When this happens, use reflections to summarize some of the key points of your discussion and plan to talk again at another time.

Use this time away to think through your strategies – what did you try that didn't work, how did you (verbally and non-verbally) handle your teen's difficult behaviors, what strategies can you try next time. Come back and re-read sections of this book to gain a greater understanding of the strategies and how you might use them.

■ ■ ■

Chapter 19 – Where to Start

✓ Try role-play practice with friends, or consider talking it through with a trained health care provider or counselor to get their input.

✓ When you have an extremely difficult teen, focus your time with them on building the trust in your relationship, discussing what is important to them, and exploring their concerns about why they don't want to talk about or consider changing a particular risky behavior.

✓ Try different strategies to find the ones that work best to overcome difficult behaviors you encounter with your son or daughter.

Final Thoughts

As hard as it may be, when having real discussions with your teen, leave your day at the door! Teens have tremendously sensitive antennae that absorb our attitudes. They know how to interpret our looks, body posture and language. They know when we are focused and when we are distracted and they know when we are just going through the motions by not offering eye contact but instead eyeing our computers, the sink full of dishes, or their screaming sibling.

They feel it personally when our cell phone rings and we allow interruptions to shift our attention. I have spent a lot of time talking through verbal communication strategies, yet your non-verbal behaviors (both conscious and unconscious) can make or break your interaction with your daughter or son.

As you know, **non-verbal communication** is the process of sending and receiving wordless cues. Your non-verbal behaviors are very important, particularly when using the strategies discussed in handling difficult behaviors (Chapters 17-19). Non-verbal communication encompasses body language, eye contact, facial expressions, and gestures. Even speech includes some non-verbal elements such as tone of voice, pitch, rate and speaking style.

Non-verbal communication represents two-thirds of all communication. The wrong message can be sent if your non-verbal and verbal communication don't match. Your non-verbal behaviors can help you to create the spirit of MI within your interaction, and can help increase the level of trust and honesty in your relationship.

Teens frequently forget what you say or do, but they rarely forget how you make them feel.

I have used examples throughout this book of ways to talk with your son or daughter that will help foster your relationship and help to move them toward positive behavior change and behavior choices. I have not shied away from sensitive topics – many of the examples I used throughout the book are things you are going to hear and should prepare yourself to respond to without freaking out. I've tried to include the variety of values and perspectives we all have as parents. You may or may not agree with all of the scenarios and examples I have shared throughout the book. That is OK – we are all different.

The strategies shared will work with many different situations. Replace my examples with ones you are dealing with or want to prepare to deal with. Please take and use the strategies that you feel will work best for you in fostering real talks between you and your son or daughter and start with those. Parenting is a process and we are growing and learning almost as much as our teens are during this time.

■ ■ ■

≫ Key Points...

Here are some key points to remember as you start using the strategies described in this book:

- **Listening** is vital to establishing a mutual, respectful relationship. Your role should be to facilitate conversations, not lead them.
- Finding opportunities for **family time** (without electronics) is critical to establishing a strong relationship with your teen.
- When having a discussion on risky behaviors, reflect on whether or not it is the **right time and place**. Make sure you are in the right frame of mind and somewhere with few interruptions.
- When teens have the opportunity to **think through and voice** their reasons and motivations for a behavior, they are more likely to follow through with them.
- **Planning for behavior change** is key to your son or daughter acting on these plans when difficult or risky situations arise.
- **Try 1 or 2 new strategies** that feel comfortable to you and build from there - you don't have to do everything all at once.

- **Give yourself a break!** Your son or daughter has no idea what new strategies you are trying to use. No one is there saying, *"That wasn't right!"* If you don't use a strategy entirely correctly, no harm is done. Try again next time. The more you practice and try out new strategies, the easier they will become.

Congratulations, you are now more equipped to handle difficult discussions with your teen! I'm so excited for you – you are on your way to establishing (or strengthening) your relationship with your son or daughter.

Don't give up. Having a strong relationship that supports real discussions about risky behaviors will make a positive impact on your teen's health and well-being. You are building a strong connection that will last beyond their teen years, ensuring you remain a trusted adviser well after they leave those years behind and become young adults!

Parent and Teen Resources

In addition to practicing the communication strategies outlined in this book, you may also be thinking – where can I find more information on some of the most common behaviors, feelings and experiences I may need or want to discuss with my son or daughter? I have compiled a list of web resources for you (and your teen) to find more information.

On the following pages, you will find general information for parents, as well as resources for both parents and teens alphabetized by category of risk.

■ ■ ■

General Information for Parents

» Centers for Disease Control and Prevention http://www.cdc.gov/parents

» U.S. Department of Health and Human Services: Office of Adolescent Health

» http://www.hhs.gov/ash/oah/resources-and-publications/info/parents/

» Society for Adolescent Health and Medicine

» http://www.adolescenthealth.org/About-SAHM/Health-Info-for-Parents-Teens.aspx

Specific Topics for Parents and Teens

Alcohol Use

For Parents:

» http://pubs.niaaa.nih.gov/publications/MakeADiff_HTML/makediff.htm#Talkingwith

» https://www.samhsa.gov/underage-drinking/parent-resources

» Parents' Drug Free Hotline: 1-855-DRUGFREE (1-855-378-4373)

For Teens:

» https://teens.drugabuse.gov/drug-facts/alcohol

» National Council on Alcohol 1-800-NCA-CALL (800-622-2255)

» National Alcohol/Drug Abuse Hotline: 1-800-662-HELP (4357)

Anger

For Parents:

» https://childmind.org/article/angry-kids-dealing-with-explosive-behavior/

» http://teenshealth.org/teen/your_mind/emotions/deal_with_anger.html

For Teens:

» https://youngminds.org.uk/find-help/feelings-and-symptoms/anger/

» http://teenshealth.org/teen/your_mind/emotions/deal_with_anger.html

Anxiety

For Parents:

» http://kidshealth.org/parent/positive/talk/anxiety_disorders.html

» http://www.childmind.org/en/posts/articles/2010-11-24-how-parent-anxious-kids

» http://www.childmind.org/en/posts/articles/2014-3-18-help-my-teen-stopped-talking-me

For Teens:

» http://youth.anxietybc.com/

» http://teenshealth.org/teen/your_mind/mental_health/anxiety.html

Binge Drinking

For Parents:

» http://www.collegedrinkingprevention.gov/media/FINALParents.pdf

» http://pubs.niaaa.nih.gov/publications/MakeADiff_HTML/makediff.htm#Talkingwith

» Parents' Drug Free Hotline: 1-855-DRUGFREE (1-855-378-4373)

For Teens:

» http://teenshealth.org/teen/drug_alcohol/alcohol/binge_drink.html

» https://www.collegedrinkingprevention.gov/parentsandstudents/students/default.aspx

» National Council on Alcohol 1-800-NCA-CALL (800-622-2255)

» National Alcohol/Drug Abuse Hotline: 1-800-662-HELP (4357)

Bullying

For Parents:

» http://kidshealth.org/parent/emotions/behavior/bullies.html

» http://www.stopbullying.gov/what-you-can-do/parents/index.html

For Teens:

» http://teenshealth.org/teen/your_mind/problems/bullies.html

» http://www.pacerteensagainstbullying.org/

Dating Violence

For Parents:

» http://www.thehotline.org/2014/02/signs-your-teen-may-be-in-an-abusive-relationship/

» http://www.loveisrespect.org/is-this-abuse/is-this-abuse

» National Domestic Violence Hotline: 1-800-799-SAFE (7233)

» National Teen Dating Abuse Hotline: 1-866-331-9474

Dating Violence (Continued)

For Teens:

» http://www.loveisrespect.org/is-this-abuse/is-this-abuse

» https://www.scarleteen.com/resource/teen_dating_violence

» National Domestic Violence Hotline: 1-800-799-SAFE (7233)

» National Teen Dating Abuse Hotline: 1-866-331-9474

Depression

For Parents:

» https://childmind.org/article/how-to-help-your-depressed-teenager/

» http://www.nimh.nih.gov/health/topics/depression/depression-in-children-and-adolescents.shtml

» National Suicide Prevention Lifeline 1-800-273-TALK (8255)

» Boys Town National Hotline (all youth, not just boys): 1-800-448-3000

For Teens:

» http://teenshealth.org/teen/your_mind/mental_health/depression.html

» http://www.helpguide.org/articles/depression/teenagers-guide-to-depression.htm

» National Suicide Prevention Lifeline 1-800-273-TALK (8255)

» Boys Town National Hotline (all youth, not just boys): 1-800-448-3000

» Your Life Your Voice Text Messaging: Text VOICE to 20121 to start

Distracted/Drunk Driving

For Parents:

» http://www.cdc.gov/parentsarethekey/

» https://www.pta.org/home/family-resources/safety/Teen-Driver-Safety/Texting-While-Driving-Parents-Role-in-Prevention

For Teens:

» http://www.t-driver.com/the-problem/driving-under-the-influence/

» http://www.distraction.gov/take-action/teens.html

» National Alcohol/Drug Abuse Hotline: 1-800-662-HELP (4357)

Drug Use

For Parents:

» http://www.drugabuse.gov/parents-educators

» http://teens.drugabuse.gov/parents

» Parents' Drug Free Hotline: 1-855-DRUGFREE (1-855-378-4373)

» National Alcohol/Drug Abuse Hotline: 1-800-662-HELP (4357)

For Teens:

» http://teens.drugabuse.gov/facts/index.php

» http://www.abovetheinfluence.com/

» National Alcohol/Drug Abuse Hotline: 1-800-662-HELP (4357)

Eating Disorders

For Parents:

» http://kidshealth.org/parent/emotions/feelings/eating_disorders.html

» http://www.nationaleatingdisorders.org/

» National Association of Anorexia Nervosa and Associated Disorders: 1-630-577-1330

» National Eating Disorders Association: 1-800-931-2237

For Teens:

» http://teenshealth.org/teen/food_fitness/problems/eat_disorder.html

» http://teenshealth.org/teen/your_body/take_care/healthy_weight.html

» National Association of Anorexia Nervosa and Associated Disorders: 1-630-577-1330

Helmet Use

For Parents:

» http://www.nhtsa.gov/staticfiles/nti/bicycles/pdf/8019_Fitting-A-Helmet.pdf

» http://www.rei.com/learn/expert-advice/bicycle-helmet.html

» http://kidshealth.org/parent/_summerspotlight/_parks/bike_safety.html

Helmet Use (Continued)

For Teens:

» http://www.nhtsa.gov/staticfiles/nti/bicycles/pdf/8019_Fitting-A-Helmet.pdf

» http://teenshealth.org/teen/safety/safebasics/bike_safety.html

» http://www.rei.com/learn/expert-advice/bicycle-helmet.html

Seatbelt Use

For Parents:

» https://www.nhtsa.gov/road-safety/teen-driving

» https://www.nhtsa.gov/risky-driving/seat-belts

For Teens:

» http://www.teendriversource.org/teen

Sex

For Parents:

» http://www.talkwithyourkids.org

» https://advocatesforyouth.org/resources-tools/?_sft_audience=for-parents

For Teens:

» http://stayteen.org/

» http://www.sexetc.org/topic/sex

» http://www.scarleteen.com/

Sex – Safer Practices

For Parents:

» http://bedsider.org/methods

» U.S. Centers for Disease Control and Prevention, AIDS/STI Hotline: 1-800-CDC-INFO (232-4636)

» Planned Parenthood: 1-800-230-PLAN (7526)

Sex – Safer Practices (Continued)

For Teens:

» http://bedsider.org/methods
» http://www.itsyoursexlife.com/stds-testing-gyt
» U.S. Centers for Disease Control and Prevention, AIDS/STI Hotline: 1-800-CDC-INFO (232-4636)
» Planned Parenthood: 1-800-230-PLAN (7526)

Sexual Orientation and Identity

For Parents:

» http://community.pflag.org/
» http://www.cdc.gov/lgbthealth/youth.htm

For Teens:

» http://teenshealth.org/teen/sexual_health/guys/sexual_orientation.html
» http://www.thetrevorproject.org/pages/programs-services
» Gay, Lesbian, Bisexual, And Transgender (GLBT) Youth Support Line: 1-888-843-4564 or the Youth Talkline 1-800-246-PRIDE (7743)
» The Trevor Lifeline: 1-866-488-7386

Suicidal Thoughts

For Parents:

» http://jasonfoundation.com/prp/
» https://suicidepreventionlifeline.org/talk-to-someone-now/
» National Suicide Prevention Lifeline 1-800-273-TALK (8255)
» Boys Town National Hotline (all youth, not just boys): 1-800-448-3000

For Teens:

» http://teenshealth.org/teen/your_mind/feeling_sad/suicide.html
» https://suicidepreventionlifeline.org/talk-to-someone-now/
» National Suicide Prevention Lifeline 1-800-273-TALK (8255)
» Boys Town National Hotline (all youth, not just boys): 1-800-448-3000

Tobacco Use

For Parents:

» http://www.lung.org/stop-smoking/smoking-facts/tips-for-talking-to-kids.html
» http://www.mayoclinic.org/healthy-living/tween-and-teen-health/in-depth/teen-smoking/art-20046474

For Teens:

» http://teenshealth.org/teen/drug_alcohol/tobacco/quit_smoking.html
» http://greatist.com/health/ultimate-guide-quitting-smoking
» Tobacco quit line, National Cancer Institute: 1-877-44U-QUIT (1-877-448-7848)

Where This Information Came From

When writing this book, I drew from a variety of resources and my years of experience as a motivational interviewing trainer, a clinician, and a mom.

These resources include:

» American Academy of Pediatrics. Bright futures tool and resource kit.

» Centers for Disease Control and Prevention [CDC] web-based resources on adolescent risky behaviors.

» Frankowski, B. L. (2009). *Strength-based interviewing*. Adolescent Medicine: State of the Art Reviews.

» Institute of Medicine and National Research Council. (2011). *The Science of Adolescent Risk-Taking Workshop Report*. Washington, DC: Institute of Medicine and National Research Council: The National Academies Press.

» Ginsburg, K. R. and Kinsman S. B. (2014). *Reaching Teens*. Strength-Based Communication Strategies to Build Resilience and Support Healthy Adolescent Development.

» McNeely, C. and Blanchard, J. (2009). *The Teen Years Explained: A Guide to Healthy Adolescent Development*. John Hopkins Bloomberg School of

Public Health, Center for Adolescent Health.

» Michigan Department of Health and Human Services (2009). *Out and Healthy: Best Practices for Working with LGBTQ Youth*. Health Professionals Resource Kit.

» Miller, W. and Rollnick, S. (2011). The Guild Press. *Motivational Interviewing: Preparing People for Change.*

» Naar-King, S. and Suarez, M. (2011). The Guild Press. *Motivational Interviewing with Adolescents and Young Adults.*

» National Institute of Mental Health (2011). The Teen Brain: Still Under Construction.

» Reclaiming Youth International: *Equipping Adults to Work With Today's Youth.*

» U.S. Department of Health & Human Services: Agency for Healthcare Research and Quality. Guide to clinical preventive services, 2014.

» U.S. Department of Health & Human Services: HRSA Maternal and Child Health web-based resources on adolescent development.

» U.S. Department of Health and Human Services: Office of Adolescent Health online learning course on adolescent development.

Printed in Poland
by Amazon Fulfillment
Poland Sp. z o.o., Wrocław

54258521R00098